CONTENTS

BET, BUILD, GO

Build Startups Like a Poker Player

Derek Kwan

To my wife Lisa, who thinks I probably should have gotten an editor...

CHAPTER 1: A GAME OF SKILL

Building a startup is one of the most difficult undertakings in the business world, but can be massively rewarding if you can succeed. It is the ultimate high risk, high reward endeavor. Finding a small team of people to get in the trenches with you, build a product from scratch, identify early adopters, and then scale a company is a lot harder than it looks. There are so many factors to consider, unknowns to deal with, and surprise failures that can completely sink your company at any time. It takes grit and endurance to survive, as well as the ability to make decisions under uncertainty. You must move quickly, while at the same time keeping mistakes to a minimum. And you have to be able to put out fires constantly, while also keeping the team focused on a long term vision. This is why even some of the most seasoned big company executives can struggle when joining an early stage startup–it really is a challenging environment unlike any other, and the skill sets needed to thrive can be broad and not well defined.

To succeed at startups, you cannot simply take the blueprint from another successful company and try to make it your own. While there are some frameworks for setting a vision, strategy, and business plan, things can be extremely situational and you will need to constantly adapt to change on the fly. It is critical to come up with innovative and sometimes contrarian ideas that reimagine how problems can be solved, while making decisions quickly and decisively with imperfect information. And you can do everything right and still suffer multiple setbacks, so you must also be resilient, even in the hardest of times.

So what does this have to do with poker? There are many commonalities between the skills required to make you a successful poker player, and those that make you successful at startups. As a matter of fact, the amount of calculated risk taking that is needed to succeed at poker *does not happen enough* at many startups. The speed of decision making required when making a tough call on a big poker hand is not something that comes easily. There is an enormous amount of study, preparation, and practice that allows players to excel at this. So we can all learn a lot from how good poker players think and prepare and execute. But first, let's define what poker is, and what poker isn't, with a story about... blackjack.

A Game Of Chance

In 1979, students from MIT and Harvard got together and formed teams to utilize card counting techniques to beat casinos at the game of blackjack. This was certainly a risky endeavor, as casinos don't take too kindly to players trying to cheat their games. The most famous team was led by Bill Kaplan, a Harvard alumnus, and J.P. Massar, a professional blackjack player, who together made a 35x return on investment in less than nine months from their exploits[1]. This is an incredible feat, as blackjack, like most casino games, is designed so that players cannot consistently make a profit in the long run. Their team was (loosely) immortalized in the 2008 movie *21*, starring Kevin Spacey, which was itself based on the best-selling book *Bringing Down the House* by Ben Mezrich.

Blackjack is a card game where players wager money with the objective of trying to get the sum of their cards as close to 21 as possible, without going over 21. Players win when the total of their cards is closer to 21 than the dealer, who represents the "house" (i.e. the casino). Players do not play against each other, only against the dealer.

Card counting is a tactic that improves a player's chances of "guessing" what the next cards will be, or more technically, the probability that a range of cards will be dealt in the future. So for example, if a player needs a 9 to make the sum of their cards equal to 21, it's a big advantage to the player if they can more accurately guess if the next card will be a 9 or something close, like a 7, 8, or 10. Players can then play more or less aggressively, and alter their bet sizing to maximize win rate and returns. As an example, if a player was dealt two cards equalling 16 in value, and they also knew there was a high probability that the next card would be something low, like a 3, 4, or a 5, the player would be much more likely to take another card, as it would get closer to 21 without going over. If the player knew the next card might be something high, like a 9 or a 10, then they would most likely not take another card, and take their chances with 16.

While card counting itself was never explicitly illegal, using counting devices or teams was certainly illegal, and could get you banned and / or arrested. There were also uncorroborated stories of cheaters getting "roughed up" in the back rooms of casinos, which added another element of potentially painful risk. The teams from Harvard and MIT were solidly in the illegal camp, working in groups and observing tables, and then signalling to each other when tables were "hot", meaning enough cards had been removed to make it easier to predict if the next cards would be high or low. Then the players would move to the "hot" tables and start betting larger amounts of money. This wouldn't work 100% of the time, as these were just probabilities, not certainties, but it did work consistently enough to yield a lot of profit.

There is an important point that might possibly be lost in this fascinating story of math and degeneracy. Although players could skirt the rules by using probability to make better guesses at cards being dealt, *they could not actually change the outcome of the hands*. After the cards were dealt and bets were made, the dealer's hand would be revealed, and the best hands would win. If players were closer to 21 than the dealer without exceeding 21, the players would win, and vice versa. The concept is similar in almost all other games in the casino, like roulette, craps, and slot machines: the player can do nothing to change the outcome of a particular hand, spin, or roll of the dice. Winners win, and losers lose, and what determines a winning or losing hand is out of the control of the players. This is the definition of a *game of chance*. These teams of players only found a way to get an extra edge that other players could not, but they could not actually change the outcome based on the rules of the game.

Of course, casinos are a business, and no casino would run and host a game that they would consistently lose in. So all these games of chance are set up in a way that players cannot exceed a 50% win rate (which is break even). For example, you can play black or red on a roulette wheel, which seems like a 50/50 chance. But it's not really 50/50, because the numbers 0 and 00 are *green*, which means there are 38 total numbers: 18 black, 18 red, and 2 green, which makes your probability of hitting black or red 47% (18/38). In fact, every bet you make on these games have known probabilities, and obviously known outcomes. These casino games are designed so that players in aggregate are constantly losing at a slight percentage, which prints money for these casinos year round, but still allows players to win enough to keep coming back. So treat your money in casinos like an entertainment expense, and not in any way like an investment when you play these casino games. Playing with friends over some cocktails is still a lot of fun, and a great way to spend a vacation. But these are certainly not games where you can in any way control the outcome.

A Game Of Skill

There are other wagering games that are considered a *game of skill*. These can be defined as games where skill overrides chance in determining the outcome of a game. Some games included in this definition are fantasy football, pool, and darts. The categorization of skill vs chance is an important one, because it can determine the legality of games for wagering in specific states in the USA. However, the determination still tends to be quite a subjective ruling when left up to politicians who are not equipped to understand the differences. In actuality, most politicians are unwilling to even entertain that differences exist at all.

A game that unequivocally falls into the *game of skill* categorization is poker. Although poker is played with cards just like other casino games, there are two important differences. First, the players are playing against each other, not against the casino. So the casino does not make money by beating players, but rather by collecting fees from hosting the games. Second, the best hand does not always win, because players can be bluffed into folding a better hand. For example, a player can have a better hand than their opponent, and if both players were to just turn their cards face up, the better hand would win. However, a player can play their hand in certain ways to make their opponent think they are beaten (i.e., bluffing), and make that opponent fold a better hand.

Good players can also find ways to minimize the money they lose for losing hands, while maximizing the amount they win for winning hands. These tactics, when done correctly and consistently, can show tremendous profit in the long run. The evidence of this skill can be seen by the same group of professional players who seem to win year after year. These skilled players have learned things that others haven't, taken an enormous amount of time to work on their craft, and are armed with sharp instincts that allow them to consistently rise to the top.

This is not to say that luck doesn't have an impact on poker. As a matter of fact, on any single day, luck will have a major impact on your wins and losses. You can do everything correctly, and still lose over and over again. As an example, one of the best starting hands in No Limit Hold 'Em poker, Ace King (AK), will still lose 32% of the time against the worst starting hand in poker, 72. So 32% of the time you induce a player to commit all their money with the worst starting hand in poker while you have AK, you will still lose. This means you can lose the next 10 times in a row with AK vs 72, and this would be a perfectly normal thing to happen. For frame of reference, here are some other probabilities in real life[2]:

1. Catching a foul ball: .12%
2. Being ambidextrous: 1%
3. A millennial becoming a millionaire: 1.8%
4. Having a lost letter returned: 3%
5. Getting food poisoning: 16%
6. Dying of heart disease: 25%
7. *Losing AK to 72: 32%*

You can see how comparatively you can lose quite frequently in poker even though you made the right decision. However, if you can induce players into this exact scenario over thousands of hands, you will eventually find yourself winning much closer to 68% of the time, and also find yourself with a much larger share of the money. This example is why discipline, a long term view, and not being results oriented are such important attributes in winning poker players.

Lastly, poker is not exactly like how it's glorified in books and movies. It's not a game where two people stare intently at each other waiting for the other to blink or fidget, which would indicate some sort of weakness to exploit. You also don't go outside for an old Western shootout in the streets at high noon because you lost a big pot (thankfully). The game is now highly based on game theory, strategy, and discipline, with still a small amount of watching for physical patterns that might indicate weakness or strength.

So poker *is* a game that you can win consistently at, and can be treated as an investment. Your return on investment will be based on your willingness to commit time and resources to learning and improving. It will depend on your capability to make good decisions and stay disciplined with your play, as well as with your bankroll. It will lean heavily on your ability to make calculated risks without all the information, and betting on these risks persistently. Then, when prioritizing and considering risk, while under sometimes overwhelming time and monetary pressure, being able to identify and make the proper trade-offs. Additionally, it will require taking a long term and strategic view of your goals to ensure success.

Building a startup, just like poker, is most certainly a *game of skill*, even if sometimes, you need a little luck to succeed. This book will use the most popular variant of poker, No Limit Hold 'Em, to draw comparisons between the skills needed to succeed in poker, with the skills needed to succeed in startups. In No Limit Hold 'Em (NLHE), players attempt to make the best "five card hand" to beat their opponents. This means that the player who can make the strongest hand with five total cards will win. Each hand of NLHE consists of two cards dealt to each player face down, or hidden, which are called "hole cards". Then five cards are dealt on the board that anyone can use (community cards):

1. Round 1 (the flop): three cards
2. Round 2 (the turn): one card
3. Round 3 (the river): one card

In each round, players are given the option to bet chips. After the river, the players will use the best combination of five total cards between their hole cards and the community cards to make the best hand. The best hand is determined by the following rankings, with the strongest hand first:

1. Royal flush: A, K, Q, J, T, all the same suit
2. Straight flush: Any five cards in a sequence, all in the same suit

(9♠ 8♠ 7♠ 6♠ 5♠)

3. Four of a kind: All four cards of the same value (AAAA)
4. Full house: Three of the same value, with a pair of different value (AAAKK)
5. Flush: Any five cards, all in the same suit (A♠ 9♠ 5♠ 3♠ 2♠)
6. Straight: Any five cards in a sequence (98765)
7. Three of a kind: Three cards of the same value (AAA)
8. Two pair: (AAKK)
9. One pair: (AA)

10. High card: None of the above, with the highest value card winning the hand

An example hand below:

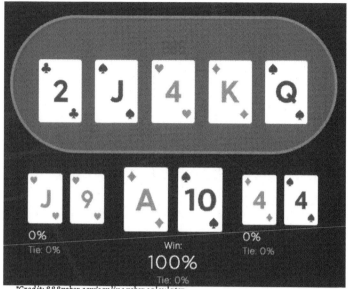

Credit: 888poker.com's online poker calculator

Throughout the book, we will refer to poker hands by using the first letter of the card (ex: AA = Ace Ace). In this example, the winning hand is AT (Ace Ten), which combined with the K (King), Q (Queen), J (Jack) on the community card "board", makes a straight, which is five cards in consecutive order (A, K, Q, J, T). The second best hand (which doesn't win anything) is the 44, which makes a "set", which is three of a kind. The KQ completes this player's hand, as those are the two highest value cards remaining, for a complete hand of 4, 4, 4, K, Q. The last place hand is the J9, which only makes a pair of Jacks, for a complete hand of J, J, K, Q, 9.

You don't need to fully understand poker to

read this book, but a little context on how the game is played will be pretty useful.

Building Startups

When you are a startup trying to differentiate your offering and disrupt incumbents, building the right product for your users is only one piece of the puzzle. You must also continuously use good judgement and critical thinking to make decisions. Solutions cannot solve one problem and create three others, so decisions need to be thought through, and second and tertiary order effects understood. Poor decision making, especially from leadership, is demoralizing to the organization, and will be a direct path to failure.

At the same time, you must move quickly and be adaptable to change, without compromising the quality of your decisions. One of the biggest advantages startups have over bigger companies is speed. When you achieve a certain size and scale, the processes that were put in place to drive efficiency will also make it difficult to change course. The organization grows both vertically and horizontally, with layers of management added to provide guidance and oversight to an ever expanding team (vertical), and more specialized departments added to keep everyone focused, as well as competing better and achieving scale by finding experts at particular job functions (horizontal). Decisions take much longer to make as there are so many people, siloed dependencies, and competing priorities, causing both approvals and cross-team communication to drag on for sometimes months. These are not inherently bad things–protecting a position after you have achieved massive scale is a success that many companies can only dream of.

Besides organizational considerations, there are also stronger customer expectations from a larger installed base of users, as users become accustomed to products working in specific ways, and solving specific use cases. There are also short term revenue expectations from shareholders for public companies, making it even harder to change product direction, as pivots tend to be costly. Lastly, politics often unfortunately plays a big role in how decisions are made at bigger companies, slowing things down (or stopping things completely) for various reasons. Startups should have very few of these restrictions, so beating incumbents in meeting shifting behaviors in a market is a huge competitive advantage, and has historically been an important lever in the disruption of incumbent markets.

Moving quickly while still making good decisions means you are taking calculated risks constantly, because you are not waiting for complete information (which oftentimes will not be possible) before making a call on something. Slow decision makers are often risk-averse, and will not commit to decisions before having as much information as possible. This type of thinking will paralyze organizations and sometimes lead to iterative decisions instead of making big bets, which will allow competitors to leapfrog you and leave you behind. So a risk-taking mindset is also required to succeed at startups. The best start-ups are adept at making good decisions and big bets with incomplete information. Furthermore, building products with lean methodologies that focus on getting lightweight proof-of-concepts in front of users will quickly raise your chances to succeed. Users can behave in unexpected ways, and will have shifting behaviors and needs. So taking too long to build a seemingly "complete" product for users can backfire, as that time could have been better spent observing and measuring to help decide what to actually build next. Hypothesis testing quickly and persistently is typically the optimal way to achieve product / market fit. Lastly, taking too long to get to market will ensure your competitors will be grabbing market share before you are even in the picture.

When a good framework is established and processes are working well, staying disciplined despite temporary setbacks is the next important puzzle piece. Jumping at temporary outcomes is just another flavor of bad decision making. The correct process, procured by critical thinking, will lead to good outcomes in the long run. Short term bad, or good, outcomes may be just variance, so focusing on making the best decisions possible is the only thing you should seek to control. A good framework for decision making will see good, repeatable results start to emerge in the long run. So being process oriented instead of results oriented, and being resilient against failure and setbacks, are strong indicators of a startup that can win the marathon. Lastly, taking a long term view on strategy and decisions will give the organization direction and context, prevent reactive thinking, and will future-proof the things you build.

Even with a good framework in place, and a culture of being process oriented and focused on the long term, judgment is still needed. Sometimes, you should take a lot longer for a decision, and wait for more data. Sometimes you do need to react, and take a short term win to keep you in the game for longer to eventually see the long term payoff. Sometimes, a proof-of-concept will not be sufficient to get traction on user adoption. Therefore, it is important to use critical thinking and judgement to utilize the pieces that make sense for a particular situation. Similarly, the best poker players have a number of tools in their toolbox, but only deploy the ones needed for specific situations. They take the time to learn everything they can, test their hypothesis at the tables, talk strategy with other players, and then relentlessly execute the things that make sense.

Even business professionals that aren't involved with startups can take away a lot from learning this framework. Big companies can apply certain principles to make themselves more adaptive to change, more tolerant of risk, and more willing to innovate in structured environments where iterative strategies designed to protect a position in the market tend to persist. Industry giants that don't adapt quickly enough when trends shift may allow feisty startups to not only steal market share, but be completely displaced in areas that might have been viewed as undisruptable by everyone.

Those who want to learn more about startups, those working in startups or who would like to, and poker professionals who want to learn more about the business world will get a lot of value from this book. Anyone who wants to learn more about poker can also take away some learnings, but the poker strategies and examples in this book will be fairly basic in nature, as they are used only in the context of teaching a different way of thinking when trying to build and scale a startup, rather than teach you how to compete with top professionals.

CHAPTER 2:
KNOW YOUR
USERS

One common misconception when building a product for a startup is that you should start with market sizing, financial projections, or other quantitative measures. Starting with numbers may help identify opportunities, but it does not start with focusing on users, and trying to solve user specific needs and problems. Building great products requires a desire to solve a real problem, preferably one that impacts and bothers the individual founders. Using analysis to find some untapped markets might help you identify and create some bottom feeding products that can gain you some short term revenue, but it would be unlikely to be a society changing solution for people. After you have identified a user problem you would really like to solve, but before you actually get started, running some quantitative analysis to see if the idea is worth pursuing would still be a good idea. But thinking through user needs and opportunities first will yield the best results. Then, if the idea passes the market size potential test, you can push forward and begin thinking through how to build solutions, and also the goals and metrics that represent a successful deployment. This order of operations is a good framework to follow for ideating great products.

The most successful companies started with a user thesis first and foremost, and often took several iterations to get to the right solution. Many ended up in a slightly different category, or pivoted their idea to handle a slightly different use case. But they started with obsessing over users first, and continued to obsess over them until their users eventually led them down the correct path. If you need more evidence on the importance of deeply understanding users, many investors love founders who are trying to solve a problem for themselves, as it implies the founders have domain expertise in the work they are undertaking. Put another way, founders who solve problems for themselves are actual users of their own solution, so they have already arrived at a deep understanding of needs and pain points. Sometimes when you are interacting with a product that does a lot of "little things" right that surprise and delight you, there are likely founders behind that product that understand you, your behaviors, needs, and pain points very deeply.

Just because you elegantly solved some user pain points on the first iteration of your product, it doesn't mean you can lose focus on your users and move on to other things. User studies are a lifelong commitment, as their behaviors and tendencies will change over time, as they adapt to movement in technology, society, your competitors, and a myriad of other factors. Users of your product today may be unrecognizable from the users of your product a year from now. You must never stop working to delight them with your product. If you do not keep a pulse on your users with constant communication via social media, surveys, customer service, and even meeting them in person, someone else will address their changing needs for you.

The Downfall Of Blockbuster

Blockbuster Video at its peak in 2004 had 84,000 employees, 9,000 stores, and was making $5.9 billion in revenue[3]. Their brand was synonymous with video rentals and became a centerpiece for what Americans did on a Friday night. It really did become part of American culture during that time. However, 10 years later, Blockbuster was down to 300 stores and their revenue had dropped to $120 million, as customers fled elsewhere for their home entertainment. It was an incredible turnaround in the wrong direction by one of the most dominant entertainment companies in the world.

The myth goes that Blockbuster's demise started in 1997, when Reed Hastings was assessed a $40 late fee when returning *Apollo 13*. Two years later, Hastings founded Netflix, and the rest is history. But Blockbuster's downfall was much more complicated than this deliciously spiteful little anecdote. One of the first falling dominoes was the rise of DVDs, which introduced threats from retailers like Walmart and Best Buy, who could sell DVDs for the same cost as a rental. Some posited that this was the biggest threat to Blockbuster in the early days. Why would customers rent something they could own for the same price? But subsequently, the rise of DVDs also sprouted new markets, making the DVD-by-mail business (Netflix) and the movie vending machine business (RedBox) economically viable. It was less costly in price and also in United States Postal Service resources to mail a DVD than a videotape. You could also fit a lot more DVD inventory into a vending machine, giving users a much wider selection of movies to choose from. So with Redbox machines in front of many grocery stores, convenience stores, and pharmacies, why make a second stop at Blockbuster when you could rent a movie after finishing running your errands? Or better yet, just pick something online and have it mailed home.

Another big domino came in a hostile take-over attempt from activist investor Carl Icahn, who was at odds with then CEO John Antioco on several fronts, from compensation (in particular a $50 million bonus if there were a change in control), to a failed bid for Hollywood Video, to decision making that was growing the business but was causing mounting financial losses for the company. Antioco had objectively turned Block-buster's business around after taking the helm in 1997. He dug into the economics of how the business was being run, while also paying close attention to user feedback and market headwinds. Blockbuster was limited in the number of copies of cassette tapes they would have in store, be-cause each copy was very costly to buy ($65), so it would take about 30 rentals to break even in cost. It was financially risky for stores to stock a lot of new releases, so inventory was always sparse. This annoyed customers, because every-one wanted new releases. Antioco stepped in and negotiated a revenue share deal with the studios, so instead of paying $65 per copy of a movie, they would instead pay $1, and share 40% of the rev-enue with the studios.[4] Antioco also eventually and audaciously removed late fees, which drove more customers back to stores, but coupled with a big hit to revenue. All these initiatives started to grow Blockbuster's business, but at very high costs, with losses at one point topping $1 billion.

At the same time, Netflix and Redbox kept growing, DVD sales kept growing, and Blockbuster was being pressured by competition from all sides. The actual events leading up to and surrounding the battle between Icahn and Antioco are fuzzy, with both sides telling different versions of the story. But Icahn has stated publicly that Blockbuster's board was fully on board with the removal of Antioco as CEO, which finally happened in 2007. This also resulted in rolling back a lot of the initiatives he had pushed for during his time.

But there was one pivotal moment in the timeline that stands out. In 2000, Netflix had been steadily growing their DVD-by-mail category. However, they were also hemorrhaging money with the high costs of running their business, which included using free trials and other deals to incentivize more users to try the product, and grow their subscriber base. As losses mounted, and in financial trouble and needing help, co-founders Reed Hastings and Marc Randolph decided to do the unthinkable–they would approach Blockbuster to sell their company. The idea was that the Netflix team would offer to run their online business, where they had more domain expertise. Then, Blockbuster could focus their time running their brick-and-mortar stores, which was in their area of expertise.

The meeting did not go well. The executives

at Blockbuster seemed unconvinced that Netflix, an online business whose offering was just mailing DVDs using the US Mail service, could ever be viable. In fact, some of them seemed to question the viability of online businesses in general, claiming they would never make money. So when Netflix offered their business for $50 million at their meeting with Blockbuster, Antioco allegedly barely held back laughter as they turned Netflix away[5]. This seemed like a death sentence for Netflix, who was losing money every day and worried about keeping the company alive. But as we all know now, Netflix eventually figured it out, and fast forward to 2020, had attained a $144 billion market cap. Blockbuster on the other hand, went in the opposite direction, having gone bankrupt a decade before. Today, there still exists a parody Twitter account "The Last Blockbuster" (@loneblockbuster) which is worth a follow.

The important lesson here is that Netflix seemed to understand Blockbuster's customers better than Blockbuster did. Customers *hated* late fees, like, viscerally, yelling-at-store-clerks hatred. So Netflix made one of their product mottos "No late fees", which can still be seen on their website and apps as part of their product offerings even today. Netflix also understood the customer of the 2000's was not the same customer of the 1990's. Their behaviors and tendencies had shifted, as more and more people were getting online. One important customer insight was that people didn't seem to care as much about the immediateness of getting a new release right when it came out, if it saved them a trip to the video store. So they were perfectly happy with the convenience of ordering online on a platform that allowed them to stack rank a queue of movies, and then just wait for that new release to get to them in the mail in a few days. Blockbuster executives very much underestimated these headwinds, and did not adapt to these changes until it was too late. Antioco actually did waive late fees and started to double down on their online business (Blockbuster online), but they had already ceded too much market share to Netflix by that point. And the rest is history.

Exploitative Poker Strategy

Blockbuster losing sight of their own users, and subsequently losing sight of emerging competitors, is similar to when poker players lose sight of their own play, as well as their opponents. Not staying informed and vigilant can have a dramatic impact on your results. At the poker table, understanding your opponents is a key factor in making good decisions. This does not mean you're just looking for a facial tick or a single bead of sweat rolling down a player's cheek to give you a "tell" on how weak or strong they are. What it does mean is understanding their style of play, their patterns and behaviors, and their mental state. There are many more factors to consider of course, but knowing your opponents is a critical one.

So what exactly are we looking for? Aggressive players will have some commonalities in their play style, and the "lines" they take, which means the sequence of actions they take throughout a hand. Similarly, passive players will also show commonalities in their tendencies. So if you learn what these commonalities are, and spot a specific pattern, you can guess with a higher probability what your opponents are doing, similar to the card counters exploiting blackjack. If you see a player exhibiting a specific behavior, such as betting a large amount when they have a strong hand, you can adjust accordingly when you see them bet a smaller amount. For example, you observed an opponent bet $300 into a pot of $400 on the river (the final turn of a poker hand). 75% of the pot size is considered to be on the larger side of bet sizing. When he revealed his cards, he had a flush (all cards of the same suit), a very strong hand. You later watch this opponent bet 75% of the pot on another hand, but you don't get to see what cards he had. Then, you watch the same opponent bet 25% of the pot, a relatively small bet, and show a bluff. Even though you only observed bet sizing patterns on three hands, and one of those hands you didn't get to see his cards, it's still enough information for you to work with. Some information is always better than no information, and you are after probabilities, not complete answers. The next time the opponent bets big in a pot with you, you will factor in several data points, but you now have a good signal that this represents strength. If you were not paying attention to how your opponent was betting, you would have missed a huge detail that may have been the difference between a win and a loss. It seemed Blockbuster was not paying attention to, or at least not considering enough, the signals their users and competitors were giving them.

On the other side, you do not want to get exploited by your opponents, so standardizing your behaviors by being consistent no matter how strong or weak you are is a good tactic. A good tip for beginner players is to take the same amount of time for every decision, and bet consistently similar amounts (relative to the pot size) in most scenarios. This way, you have removed at least one signal that your opponents can use against you. Over time, as you become more comfortable with playing, you can start to mix things up against your opponents, which we'll cover in a later chapter. You can even throw "reverse tells" at observant players, such as leaning back (a sign of weakness), when you are actually strong, or covering your cards with your hand (a sign of strength), when you are actually weak.

For less experienced players, you might want to avoid directly answering any questions from professionals. Unfortunately, some table talk is actually a probe to get more information from you. Remember, a little information is better than no information, and if you are a relative unknown, a big advantage will be your anonymity. For example, pros will ask, in a friendly way, where you play, which games, and at what stakes. This might seem like casual conversation, but they are actually trying to get very specific information from you. Your stakes (how much money you play for) is particularly important, because there are dramatic differences in play styles between a high stakes vs a low stakes player. And "fitting" you into a play style and trying to exploit that will be better than nothing. However, this is not to say don't talk to people at the poker table. Poker is still a fun, social game. But just be careful with the line of questioning you get from certain people, and try to understand why they are asking you specific questions.

You may notice that in order to exploit other players, you need to be able to do two things. First, you need to observe their behaviors, so paying attention at the poker table is important. Second, you need to know what to do with these observations, which takes intense study, preparation, and practice. Just because you know someone has a strong hand, doesn't necessarily mean you know how to exploit that behavior for the maximum amount of equity. Or you may not even know what a player is doing when they take a drink of water when in the middle of a hand with you. The best poker players spend a lot of time "in the lab", studying and running through different scenarios, and comparing notes with other good players, before they go to the tables to experiment with their new tools. But then, most importantly, they will still need to exhibit intense discipline to achieve results. It's not enough to just know what to do–you also need to be able to consistently execute over long periods of time. Startups that use these same methodologies to learn about their users and competitors, commit time to thinking and learning, and then executing consistently and with discipline have a much higher chance of rising to the top.

Users Are Your Lifeblood

The biggest lesson we can take away from the success of Netflix, as well as from the habits of the best poker players, is that when starting a business, paying attention to the behaviors and needs of your users is *everything*. Without a deep understanding of what users want, their pain points, likes and dislikes, and keeping track of changes in their patterns and behaviors, you cannot possibly hope to build something that users will love, and eventually scale your business and beat your competitors. If you can get a small group of early adopters to love your product, you're off to a great start, and is in fact one of the first goals that all startups should aim for. Almost all successful companies start with a group of fervent early users, who will not only show you how to build a better product, but then also be your most effective brand ambassadors, as long as you're keeping them happy. Do anything to make these users satisfied, even things that don't scale, at least until you are much closer to product / market fit. Scale will never come unless you have happy users, so first things first.

For example, AirBnB back in 2009 seemed to have arrived at a good implementation of their vision: to facilitate the booking of homes between homeowners and guests. But the traction in those early days was a lot slower than they expected, and they couldn't really put a finger on what was happening. So the founders at AirBnb went out and personally booked and stayed with hosts in New York to see what they were missing. They discovered that hosts were generally terrible marketers–their listings had poorly shot and amatuer looking photos, causing their listings to get much less engagement. Good photos are critically important in the online travel and booking industry because users can only get an idea of their potential experience via photos on the internet. Good photos can attract more eyeballs, as well as build trust and excitement with users. So AirBnb chose to do something that would never scale: they bought a $5000 camera and individually went to homes and took pictures to help their hosts.

This caused a few things to happen: hosts were given immediate help, as their listings started to get more engagement, which led to more bookings. Other hosts, seeing the success of having professional photos taken as a best practice, learned to start paying more attention to the aesthetics of their listings. Guests were provided a more delightful experience on AirBnb's site, and started to trust the listings and book more. This all resulted in AirBnb seeing 2-3x more bookings in New York, with revenue in the city doubling in one month[6].

A good way to learn from this success story is to imagine what AirBnb might have done *wrong* instead. When they first noticed a lack of traction, they could have continued to grind away at numbers and theories from their office, instead of going to see their users in person. It is expensive financially, not to mention straining on people and their families to travel for work. It is faster to launch features and updates and have your users give you feedback *afterwards*, rather than wait to collect this information by speaking to them and observing their behavior beforehand. But so much can be lost in translation, even over the phone. Being in person allows for more natural conversation, deeper exploration, and being able to see and interpret non-verbal cues (a big skill of the best poker players). Being in person also builds relationships with users, which is great to have with your early adopters.

Another thing AirBnb could have done wrong–when they realized that hosts needed to take better pictures, they could have broadcast instructions to everyone via email or an announcement on the website on how to take better pictures–maybe some articles and videos on tips and best practices. This would have been less strenuous on finances and resources. Founders who are still trying to build their product, maintain their finances, run their teams, and a thousand other things really don't have time to go around taking pictures for people. But it is impossible to overstate how important it is to understand and serve your users in your early days. Going through the process of taking pictures for hosts will not only help them be more successful, but also help you understand in depth what struggles they have. It is only then that you can more effectively build a better process or feature to help. And you can take this general mindset and apply it to almost all your user related issues: learn who your users are, learn what their pain points are, what it would take to make them successful, and then learn what *really makes them tick* by going in person and getting to know them. There will be more background on the founding of Airbnb in a later chapter.

Your early adopters can show you the way to build a product that will get more adoption from the next wave of users, and the next wave, taking you from dozens to possibly millions of users if you take the time to really understand their needs. Their word of mouth will spread like wildfire and ignite your business, as the authenticity of user testimonials will beat any of your other marketing efforts by a long shot. The book "Crossing the Chasm" by Geoffrey Moore discusses this phenomenon in detail, with this handy "technology adoption curve" visual:

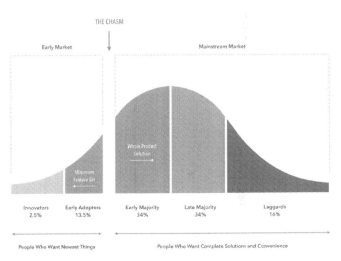

*Technology adoption curve by Geoffrey Moore, via https://smithhousedesign.com/
models-predicting-future-geoffrey-moores-crossing-chasm/

Your early adopters will help you "cross the chasm" to reach your biggest groups of "majority" users, at which point you have truly hit product / market fit and can scale. But without those early adopters, you may never cross that chasm at all, so you must ensure they love your product.

Discovering user needs is not just an exercise in asking simple questions about product usage, what they want built, and what bugs they would like fixed. This is an opportunity to get inside their minds to see how they view the world, and to uncover the optimal solutions to help them with their problems. Who are the core users of the product, and what are their goals and key issues? Why does your product matter to them? How does it help achieve their goals? What does the product do really well, and what does it do poorly, and why? What are the gaps in other solutions on the market, from the users' perspective? When watching them use your product, are they taking any crazy workarounds to do their tasks? Are there some things they want to do that they can't do at all? Only after this deep exploration into your users should you really get into your lab and start building. Answer all these questions well, and build elegant solutions to all of them, and you will be on your way to true product / market fit.

CHAPTER 3: DECISIONS AND RISK

The toughest thing about poker is that you cannot see your opponent's cards, or know what cards will be dealt next. You are constantly trying to make decisions with imperfect information. You have a strong hand, but your opponent may have a stronger hand that beats you. Or they might be completely bluffing. So when an opponent takes an aggressive action towards you, how can you know with certainty how to respond without knowing all the cards? Should you try to make a bluff, if it's possible your opponent might be trapping with a good hand? You can never really know for sure. Even worse, these tough decisions often must be made under tremendous time and monetary pressure. Even in mid-stakes poker games, thousands of dollars can depend on a single decision on a single turn in a poker hand, and you typically need to make a decision very quickly on the spot.

Some poker players seem to have this magical ability to read their opponents' hands with frightening accuracy. Except it's not magic. It's a mix of critical thinking, observation, pattern recognition, and a little math. And the end result is being able to narrow hands down to a range, and then play against that range accordingly. This is "probabilistic thinking" in a nutshell. You will rarely have all the information when making decisions, and you can't drag on decisions waiting for all the data. You will need to use whatever tools you have at your disposal to make a call, and sometimes you will be wrong. But if you keep making decisions on the correct side of probabilities, driven by your own critical thinking, observation, and measurements, the results will come, as will long term success.

If you have ever tried to build a startup in a competitive market, or even just had to make a tough call as a leader in an organization, all of this might sound familiar to you. You cannot know exactly what's going to happen with absolute certainty. You don't know if you're stepping into a trap or some other bad situation that you can't see. In startups, your financial situation is often precarious, even if you have raised a lot of capital. Your competitors are always watching, waiting for a misstep. And the pressure just doesn't seem to stop. But somehow, a small percentage of startups continue to thrive and disrupt incumbents year after year.

Calculated Risk

Making decisions under uncertainty means you are deliberately taking risks. Just like betting on a decision at a poker table, you must also bet on your decisions at a startup. Except at a startup, your decisions can have much farther reaching consequences. Startup decisions can utilize capital and resources wisely or poorly, while impacting employees, customers, investors, partners, and the broader competitive landscape. There is a tremendous amount of pressure to get decisions right, while at the same time, a critical need to make decisions quickly with imperfect information. Therefore, the application of *calculated* risk will balance speed with accuracy as you have to make tough calls under uncertainty.

So what would be a good framework to make better decisions in this kind of environment? A smart place to begin is by looking at what constitutes *bad* decisions. Guessing without trying to process whatever information is available to you, or not thinking things through logically are certainly ways to make some bad decisions. And you might be surprised how often this happens in the professional world, even at big companies. Another is the inability (or refusal) to factor in the secondary or tertiary effects of decisions. Bonus points if you're unaware of how your organization has to constantly clean up the unintended consequences of your decisions. Being reactive and not thinking big picture, and especially being reactive to small sample sizes will thrash your team. Not being able to view the world from the perspective of others, and making decisions only from your own viewpoints will often lead to bad outcomes. Not paying attention to broader trends, and an inability to use critical thinking to determine what is a fad instead of a more permanent shift in the market will lead to missed opportunities, and again, more wasted resources.

Sometimes these bad decisions will reveal to you pretty quickly that you made a bad decision. But other times, the effects will be a slow bleed– it might take a long time before you start seeing the negative impacts on your business metrics and your ability to scale, and by then it might be too late. Over time, this type of decision making can be severely damaging to your organization, as you are constantly forced to course-correct bad decisions, as well as clean up the negative consequences that will inevitably follow. This will prevent your team from staying focused and being productive in building your future. And a tendency to make bad decisions will compound, stacking one bad decision on top of another until your business is completely buried and unable to unwind itself from everything that has happened.

An alternative option would be to not make a decision at all until you have more information. This is not inherently bad, when used appropriately. Some decisions need more time, especially those that deploy a lot of resources, or those that may drastically change the direction of a strategy. But most of the time, if decision makers are constantly delaying decisions to gather more data, it will paralyze your organization, and allow competitors to leapfrog you. Allowing "pencil pushing" to be your decision mechanism is a surefire way to lead your team into obscurity, this behavior will push you to iterate instead of innovate. It will also lead to some undesirable incentives for your team, such as optimizing for certain short term KPIs, rather than focusing on long term user needs and problems. A decision with 70-80% of the information will almost always be better than having your team sit around waiting another month for 10% more data.

An 80% decision will mean that, often, "done is better than perfect". Why is this ok when building products? If you practice lean decision making, you will be more action-oriented by default, as you learn to act faster. However, a bigger factor is your ability to either *fail fast*, or *iterate quickly*. You can do neither if you wait for 100% of the information. Remember, your advantage as a startup is speed, so if your idea is going to bomb,

bomb it quickly and move on to the next idea. Don't take up a year of planning and resources to find out your idea doesn't work. Furthermore, you can never 100% predict user behavior, no matter how much research you do. Users are fickle, and they can behave in unexpected ways, and their needs will change over time. You want to get lightweight products in front of them quickly and observe their behavior so you can adapt, instead of building monolithic solutions that take too long, and may need to change anyway. You might also have a few surprises in the competitive landscape in just a few months, which can change everything about your users and your solution. Lastly, showing quick wins can boost the morale of your team. Deploying products into production is *progress*, and each delivery can be a celebration of a job well done (most of the time). Another organizational benefit is giving marketing and sales a jumpstart, who can promote things before they are complete, which can also give you another signal of potential interest.

So other than avoiding the behaviors above, or correcting them if they are already happening, what's a good framework to *take* persistent calculated risks that will deliver more upside than downside? How can we balance accuracy with speed, and ensure we don't fix one problem, but create three other problems? How can we ensure we don't let pencil pushers paralyze our decisions?

When making decisions, applying logic, critical thinking, intuition, and quantitative measures seem like obvious concepts. It can be surprising, and honestly a little frightening, how often you encounter individuals in leadership positions who don't do this well. Building a culture in which decisions are made by the "seat of your pants" will accumulate massive amounts of issues over time, in the form of:

1. Technical debt in your product, which will cripple engineering velocity over time (more on this in later chapters)
2. Frustration from smart individual contributors and middle management, as they are forced to execute decisions they know don't really make any sense, as well as damage to their own reputations
3. Wasted time and resources on your organization, as they play "whack a mole" to problems introduced by poorly thought through decisions
4. Demoralization and loss of trust from your organization, due to the previous bullet point and lingering doubt their leaders can deliver success
5. Eventual failure as your company can no longer overcome the mountain of debt and paralysis caused by poor de-

cision making

So clearly applying logic, critical thinking, intuition, and quantitative measures are necessary. But there is some nuance on when and how to apply each concept. When faced with a specific decision, think through the **risk / reward / loe** (level of effort) profile. If rewards are low, question why you are considering it in the first place. If risk is high, is the reward high enough to justify undertaking the endeavor?

	High Risk	Low Risk
High reward	You need at least one of these a year to be innovative and win	Attacking these persistently will equate to long term success
Low reward	These don't make any sense	You have better things to do

What about the amount of resources and time it will take (loe)? Will something else of equal risk / reward take less time and resources? And how do all these factors stack against other endeavors that are in the queue? Only after this analysis should you choose to deploy resources to prioritize and execute a decision. And this doesn't really need to take that much time to do.

Now that you have narrowed down the list of decisions to undertake, it's time to apply logic, critical thinking, intuition, and quantitative analysis. And primarily, you are analyzing the *risk* component, as mostly every decision you make will have some amount of risk. In areas where risks are well known, you don't have that much need to apply intuition. Logic and quantitative analysis are more important. For example, if you were deciding on opening a banana stand, this is an endeavor where risks are very well known. Do people in this area consume bananas? Check the demographics and buying patterns. Do bananas carry a high risk of violating health codes? Doesn't seem insurmountable if there are any. Do I need a lot of capital to open a banana stand? Bananas are cheap, stands are cheap, a license might be a little expensive. Are there banana stand competitors I need to watch out for? Probably just food markets, but you get to carry the novelty of being a *stand*! You don't need much intuition to answer these, almost all of them can be quantified with some web searches and applying some Fermi math here and there, and you're better off quickly using logic and moving forward with a decision than spending a lot of time thinking about it.

However, when risks are unknown, and there is a higher degree of uncertainty, intuition is more needed, as data points are harder to come by, and logic that can be extrapolated from similar problems may not be accessible here. But "winging it" with your intuition is really no different than flying by the seat of your pants, so using frameworks and heuristics to structure your intuitive thinking are necessary in making good decisions. For example, say instead of a banana stand, you wanted to build flying cars instead (and I applaud your broad range of interests). You know some of the risks of flying cars (people and vehicles falling from the sky, luddites, and government regulations), but it's quite hard to measure these risks, as you have very little precedent to lean on. Also, there are probably a lot of other risks involved with operating vehicles in the air, but it's hard to see all the non-obvious cases, as again, no one has ever done it before. But you can use some intuition for certain things. What are the potential benefits of a flying car? Should improve traffic, and flying cars are cool. Who would be the early adopters of a flying car? Seems like Tesla has possibly built a playbook here, by starting upmarket with the Model S first, but again, quite impossible to know for sure. How obstructive will the government be? They are always obstructive, but it's not hard to see how highly obstructive they would be for this, and for good reason. Would you run into line-of-sight complaints from residents, drivers, and helicopters? Probably. Generally, you can sense the big differences in knowns vs unknowns between a banana stand, and a big innovation like a flying car. You can now also see when and how to apply different models for thinking and analyzing problems. A deeper dive into applying *probabilistic thinking* in making these decisions will be covered in a later section of this chapter. So in summary, turning pure risk-taking into *calculated risks* should make such endeavors less threatening, while increasing probabilities for success if done correctly.

A good case study for a calculated risk that succeeded in a big way is Uber in their early days, when faced with the challenge of entrenched monopolies formed by the taxi industry and local city governments.

Uber Vs The Taxi Monopolies

To drive a taxi in most major cities, you need a "taxi medallion", a type of CPNC (Certificate of Public Necessity and Convenience). This falls into the realm of "occupational licensing", which restricts new entrants to select occupations without a license granted by the government. Often, these licenses are given somewhat arbitrary limits in a given area, which has secondary effects, such as restricting the mobility of workers (ex: being licensed at a nail salon in one area does not certify you for any other areas), and the creation of monopolies (ex: the taxi industry). If a given area only had a set number of licenses, it would prevent new entrants (and new ideas) from entering that area. And the consumer would suffer, as there would be no alternative to go to if the incumbents wanted to drop their quality of service or massively raise their prices.

The restriction on the number of licenses of course also drove up prices, where taxi medallions cost $25,000 each back in 1962, but ballooned to $1,000,000 each in 2013[7]. As a result, taxi drivers started taking out risky loans to acquire medallions–loans that were quite similar to the ones that caused the 2008 financial crisis, and were impossible to pay back given the earnings of the drivers. To no one's surprise, it also caused rent seeking behavior, as owners of the medallions started renting their licenses to others. This also coincidentally made the issuers (the government) a lot of money, so there was little incentive to change the system. The total value of medallions in New York City by 2013 was $16.6 billion dollars.

And then along came Uber. Uber burst onto the scene in 2009, and re-invented the ride-hailing industry. It allowed riders to hail a car from their mobile phones, and set the destination, which was an incredible upgrade to phone calls or standing by a curb waving your arms. It provided price transparency, by displaying the exact amount of fare you would pay to get to your destination. If anyone has ever been in a taxi that took the liberty of taking you on the "scenic route" to drive up your fare, you could see how important this feature was. It provided riders with the identity of their drivers, and also drivers would know the identity of their riders beforehand. Uber also provided a rating system, which would then also incentivize good behavior for all parties. It introduced ride sharing, and made it easy for strangers to share a ride while going in the same direction, and split the fares automatically. Lastly, and one of the most important impacts of Uber, is it gave rise to a technologically driven gig economy. A ton of latent supply in the market, in the form of everyday people with cars, was suddenly given a way to earn income, on their own hours, on their own terms. It was a huge win for consumers, riders and drivers alike. Regardless, Uber was heavily restricted from major cities due to the taxi medallion system. The taxis certainly didn't want the competition, and the government didn't want to lose their control and revenue source.

So Uber... just went for it anyway. And they knew exactly what they were doing– challenging the government, and what was effectively a cartel in the form of the taxi industry, by servicing cities where they were not licensed. It was the ultimate form of "ask for forgiveness, not permission". And flush with venture capital, Uber flooded cities with their drivers, and started to quickly take the market over with their superior product and service. The prices of medallions plummeted as riders turned to Uber in droves. With the rush of supply to the market, ride prices dropped, another huge win for riders. The governments weren't happy about this, and neither was the taxi industry:

> Advocates for the medallion business, including New York Mayor Bill de Blasio, have responded to the ride-hailing business with a formula already proven to fail: They want to limit the number of Uber and Lyft drivers. The city council has legislated a cap on ride-hail drivers, which Uber has challenged. Because the ride-hail model is winning in the marketplace, they want to make it more like the medallion business: that is to say, a business with artificially fixed supply.[8]

But it was too late: there was such huge adoption of Uber by the citizens of these cities that it would have been political suicide to fully try and ban them. Even with monopolistic measures pushed upon them, Uber's growth in major cities was only temporarily contained, until market forces took over and Uber won, eventually crashing the prices of medallions down to $170,000 in 2018[9].

There is a term for what Uber did: *regulatory entrepreneurship*, where disruptors spot a market inefficiency, and in some cases, a government sponsored monopoly, and try to go around regulations to serve a consumer base, with the goal of changing the laws in their favor. By taking a *cal-

culated risk to go for massive market penetration before they could be stopped, it would be too difficult for governments to try and defend these monopolies against the needs of their own citizens. This doesn't always work, but a few notable examples where it succeeded were Uber, Lyft, Tesla, Airbnb, and DraftKings.

The commonality is that there is just no way to know for sure. It's already difficult to take over a market with big incumbents backed and subsidized by the government. But then to bet that the government will just have to cave in if you get big enough? And the incumbent won't figure out a way to beat you anyway? It's a bet of massive proportions, and there is no amount of data in existence that can assure you that your bet is correct.

Probabilistic Thinking

Some poker players seem to have this magical ability to read their opponents' hands with frightening accuracy. Except it's not magic. It's a mix of critical thinking, observation, pattern recognition, and a little math. And the end result is being able to narrow hands down to a range, and then play against that range accordingly.

This is "probabilistic thinking" in a nutshell. You will rarely have all the information when making decisions, and you can't drag on decisions waiting for all the data. You will need to

DEREK KWAN

use whatever tools you have at your disposal to make a call, and sometimes you will be wrong. In reference to the section above, applying some statistical thinking, intuition, and heuristics can help you narrow down both the problem and solution spaces. The *output* of this analysis will be a decision that carries a certain *probability* that you will achieve the outcome that you want. This isn't a guarantee, it's just a likelihood that some event will happen. This explicitly means there is always a non-zero chance that your choice will lead to a bad outcome, but this does not mean your decision was incorrect. This topic will be covered thoroughly in a later chapter.

Just about every poker hand ever played applies this concept, because you cannot see your opponent's cards, and are therefore always making a judgement on your probability of winning a hand. But we can pick one fun hand to use as an example, from a poker show called "High Stakes Poker" back in 2010, where two legendary players, Phil Ivey and Tom Dwan battled one another in a pot worth almost $1 million dollars. Both players are extremely aggressive and quite adept at applying *mixed strategies*, which means they can play similar situations very differently, making them very hard to play against. We will discuss mixed strategies in a later chapter.

Tom Dwan had re-raised several players to $28,900 before the flop with a hand we'll keep hidden for now, chasing away all the other players except for Phil Ivey, who calls with the A♦6♦. On a flop of K♦Q♣T♦, Dwan bets $45,000, representing a very strong hand that connects with all those high cards, which is believable because of his big raise before the flop. Phil Ivey knows this, but also knows Dwan can be bluffing a lot here, so he calls, thinking his high card (Ace) may still be currently the best hand. Ivey can also make the best flush with one more diamond, and a straight with a Jack. The pot is now $162,300. The turn brings the 3♠, which doesn't help Ivey at all. Dwan bets again for $123,200, signifying extreme strength. Phil Ivey thinks for a little while, and makes a pretty tough call here with just Ace high and a few draws, making the pot $408,700. The river comes the 6♣, for a final board of K♦Q♣T♦3♠6♣, which now makes Ivey a pair of sixes, which is not a very strong hand here based on how aggressive Dwan has played thus far. As we mentioned earlier, you can never really know what your opponent has. Dwan goes all-in on the river (which means he bets all his remaining chips) for $268,200, making the pot $676,900. What would you do? Could you call another $268,200, making the pot almost $1 million, with just a pair of sixes?

Most players would be correct to just fold here. There is really a high number of hands that beat a pair of sixes, especially with the aggressive way Dwan played the hand. However, Dwan is also such an aggressive player that he could be completely bluffing here with absolutely nothing. The monetary pressure of such a huge pot also plays another uncomfortable factor. Ivey thought for a very long time, while Dwan sat stone faced, not moving for several long minutes, before eventually and reluctantly folding.

Phil Ivey was working out the probability that his pair of sixes would be the best hand, likely by assigning probabilities to the various hands that Dwan could have. In the end, he felt that there was a higher probability that Dwan held a hand that was better than his. There are some more advanced poker concepts at play here, such as assigning ranges of hands to your opponent, calculating how your hand does against that range, and calculating your "pot odds" (how much money do you have to call compared to how much total money you would win), as well as some psychological analysis based on a number of different factors. A deep dive into these concepts are out of scope for this book, but in summary, Ivey was applying all this analysis to determine the *probability* his hand was the best. It was impossible to know for sure, and ultimately, he determined it was not, but it was clearly a very close decision.

So what did Dwan have? Incredibly, he only had the 9 ♠ 8 ♠, which was a complete bluff, meaning Phil Ivey had folded the best hand with a pair of sixes. However, this does not mean that Phil Ivey's fold was a bad decision. And as a matter of fact, Ivey being so close to a call with such a marginal hand in an absurdly large pot shows how talented these top pros really are.

You can apply this model of probabilistic thinking to many startup decisions. Oftentimes, decisions will be straightforward with fairly known risks and outcomes. As we mentioned earlier, some rapid application of logic and statistics are appropriate in these situations. Your probability of achieving a specific outcome should be quite high, if done correctly. But there are many decisions where you can't ever know exactly what will happen. You can, however, find ways to assign a probability to an outcome, or better yet, to several outcomes.

Let's take one of our questions from a previous exercise: *Who would be the early adopters of a flying car?* You can't know for sure, but we can apply several of the discussed concepts to arrive at some potential outcomes and assign them probabilities. There is some research that shows the wealthy tend to be early product adopters.

A simple way to forecast the future is to look at what rich people have today; middle-income people will have something equivalent in 10 years, and poor people will have it in an additional decade. Think of VCRs, flat-screen TVs, mobile phones, and the like. Today, rich people have chauffeurs. In 10 years or less, middle-income drivers will be able to afford robotic cars that drive themselves, at least in some circumstances.[10]

So looks like there is some indication that the wealthy might be a good place to start. What would your early adopters be using flying cars for? A flying car can certainly be viewed as a novelty item at first launch, as there should be low inventory and a product that no one has ever seen before. This also fits into the above study–new products tend to be novel, and adopted by the wealthy more frequently. Who would definitely not be an early adopter? Technophobes and risk-averse people would be unlikely. While these traits can exist in people of any income demographic, we can definitely see this more often in older individuals. Seems like our answer is skewing greatly towards "wealthy and young". Also, the cost of goods sold for developing a flying car will be quite high in the beginning, and may get cheaper over time if you can achieve economies of scale, so it would generally make sense strategically to price your product high in the beginning. Furthermore, Tesla strategically targeted the wealthy with the Model S with great success, with base models starting at $80,000, going up to $150,000 fully loaded, and may be a good case study to model your flying car after. So now we can assign some rough probabilities to our answer:

1. Wealthy and young: 70%

2. Wealthy and old: 25%
3. Low income and young: 4%
4. Low income and old: 1%

The probability of our early adopters being wealthy and young appear quite high. What about government obstruction? It appears that a flying car would be quite risky, and would need to clear a lot of regulatory hurdles to get off the ground. Do wealthy people vote? What about young people? Young people have for a very long time been the lowest turnout for voting, with 18-29 was 19.9% in 2018, while 65+ was 59.4%. In 2018, the youth turnout improved dramatically, but still only at 35.6%, while 65+ rose to 66.1%. So it looks like young people won't help us with moving the government much. But if we peg wealth to education level, people without a high school diploma voted at 22.2% in 2014, 27.2% in 2018, while those with advanced degrees turned out 62% and 74% respectively.[11] So looks like our demographic may or may not help with pushing for changes at the government level, looks like a coin flip at 50%. So the chances of getting through government regulations quickly seems quite low.

And we can continue with more estimation questions to target a good demographic for launch, to understand the risks, and also to formulate our messaging and positioning, as well as our sales strategy. When thinking about features, we can also cater to that specific demographic more, hoping they will be market makers. There will be no guarantees, but these types of exercises can give you good estimates to understand what might be ahead of you.

Thinking probabilistically will lead to some good habits. Knowing that you are making decisions without having all the information will foster faster decisions, and less sitting around waiting for all the data. Problems before that seemed to have completely unknown solutions or outcomes can be viewed from a different light. You are not after perfect answers, and you are ok with outcomes that didn't go exactly according to plan, which will make you fear failure less. Think back to some recent problems that arose that seemed too difficult to find clear solutions for. Can you play those problems back and apply some probabilistic thinking instead? What possible outcomes are there from your decisions? Any outcomes you clearly don't want, that you can avoid ahead of time? Looking at the world probabilistically can open up incredible efficiencies in the way you process information and make decisions. All you need to do is take the time to really work through problems, and analyze whatever data you have on hand. If you can keep making decisions on the correct side of probabilities, driven by your own critical thinking, observation, and measurements, the results will come, as will long term success.

CHAPTER 4:
THE GETTING
STARTED
CHECKLIST

I f you make good bets and decisions and stay disciplined and persistent, somewhere down the line, you may find yourself with product / market fit, a big batch of daily active users, rapidly growing revenue, and a team of people working together on your idea. But how did we get here? How did we even get this off the ground?

This chapter will be a checklist of things to consider when getting a startup up and running. It will cover the major principles and things you need to sweat, while offering some brief details, or pointing to better sources of info.

Product And Market Analysis

We covered some of this in previous chapters, but focus on specific user problems, and really work through all the use cases. Ask yourself clarifying questions on what the goals of the product are, who your core users are, which specific problems are they solving for your users, how other solutions solve these same problems, and try to see what problems might exist five years from now. What are things that no one else is thinking of? Then try to measure your market size: how many potential users are there? How much would they pay for your product? And if your product is free, how else might you make money?

Founding Team Members

Most founders have a co-founder these days, typically pairing a technical person with a person good at sales / marketing / customer support / finance. But whether it's a co-founder or your first batch of 2-5 employees, what you are looking for in your early days are generalists with grit. You need to have resilient people who can wear many hats, and solve a wide array of problems that are not limited to a single job description. And they need to have "alligator blood" to fight through problems, rebound from failure, and keep grinding along. In your early days, everything will seem like a fire. You need gritty generalists to get you through.

Grit in particular is needed in your organizations to stay longer with problems. But not all problems need grit. In fact, many problems are not meaningful in the grand scheme of your business strategy and operations, and don't need attention at all.

Later down the road as you're scaling, you will need specialists more, as you learn to stop "running with scissors". Whether or not you promote from within or hire externally is entirely dependent on everyone's capabilities, and the expectations and goals that you are setting. A blend of internal and external usually works best, with the percentages a decision you can make at that time.

Team Building

As you start with a bunch of generalists with high grit, everyone will jump in and do what needs to be done, sometimes with people figuring out how to do things they have never done before. The term "build the plane while you're flying it" is quite an apt analogy for early stage startups. But as you scale to around 20 employees, some structure starts to crystalize. Your development team starts to split into different groups responsible for different parts of the product, or might be split into self-contained "pods" who each work on specific projects. If you see your engineering team moving too slow on projects, there can be multiple factors, but a very common cause is too much "thrash" in their sprints. Instead of focusing on feature development, they are pulled into bug fixing, investigations, and technical debt. Creating a support team that can serve as a "tier 1" to deflect some of this work off their queues can help them move dramatically faster. When engineers have to *context switch*, it can cause projects to explode in time spent. Other sources of context switching are pulling engineers into too many meetings, or simply just going to their desks and constantly asking them questions.

As you scale your engineering team, you also want to scale your product management team. Roughly an 8:1 (8 engineers to 1 product manager) to 10:1 ratio is about average. You also want to scale QA to about a 3:1 (3 engineers to 1 QA) to 5:1 ratio. Project managers will likely be needed as your engineering team grows to around 25-30 in total size.

Your sales, marketing, account management, and business operations and finance hires will vary based on industry and needs, but you will typically split sales into "business development" (sourcers) and "account executives" (closers). Marketing may be split into departments that are responsible for content, ads, social media, product marketing, and more. Account management can have tech support, client success strategists, phone reps, onboarding teams, and more. Financial reporting and business operations can typically be handled by generalists until you start scaling beyond a few million in revenue, in which case you will start to need dedicated specialists in those roles.

Across all of these teams, communication will be critical. Over-communication will be better than under-communication almost always, so foster an environment where everyone follows up, and holds each other accountable for what they need to do. Be professional and empathetic with communication externally and internally, and know that tone can be misinterpreted when written in words. Usually, after 2-3 back and forths on a topic, a real time message will be better than email, whether that is a chat app or a quick meeting. But err on the side of consistent and timely communication to hold everyone together.

You will tend to see some changing needs at 20, and then 50 employees (as certain labor laws start kicking in), and then 100 as you really start to scale. The need for executive leadership will start showing around 40-50 employees, but again, needs will be dependent on industry and company. This is also around the time you should be looking for dedicated human resources.

If you get lucky enough to hire a top performer, your job is to give all the context and hand over the wheel. However, if you apply this same methodology to people who are not capable, you will find yourself constantly cleaning up their messes, as well as demoralizing them. Having to micromanage certain individuals is not a failing of anyone's. It's an opportunity to provide mentorship and guidance to turn as many people as you can into top performers. Not everyone is capable, but some will be—the most important thing for all involved is arriving to a conclusion quickly. After you find those who are capable, make sure you're not just showing them *how*, but explaining to them *why*. As they grow more self-sufficient and their capability to problem solve and execute become stellar, then you can hand over the wheel to them too. And you will have been a helpful headwind in their successful journey.

There are many other hiring considerations, such as people operations, which focus on employee happiness, office perks, and company culture. Figuring out when you need some lawyers on retainer, or even in house, to help with compliance issues and potential litigation. Dedicated writers can be useful for a variety of purposes. Giving business teams their own technical resources, such as web developers, sales engineers, sales operations, and more can also help those teams be more efficient. There are a wide variety of roles that can help your company succeed, and choosing the right ones for your specific needs can help you keep hitting milestone after milestone. If you spend most of your time trying to recruit and hire the best people, taking your time to find the best hires, that might be the most important thing you can do for your company's success. On the other side, also ensure you are identifying low performers, and take corrective action *quickly*, up to and including termination. Low performers can drag down your growth and demoralize your top performers, and can poison other team members if they have bad behavior. "Hire slow, fire fast", as the saying goes.

Leadership

Good leaders create a stable environment for their team. They turn chaos into structure and a plan. They have set a mission and a vision that always serves as a persistent and guiding North Star. They ask an annoying amount of questions, rather than blurt out statements without enough context. Even when every option is terrible, they can pick the best terrible option to move forward, even if that decision might be unpopular, and maintain stoicism throughout.

The best leaders are also great mentors, and provide big picture context and thought processes and mental models, which are more important than just "blueprints". They can coach others to always seek to extrapolate from the things they learn, and see how frameworks can be applied to different scenarios. Having a manager who can also mentor will do more for career paths than any class they can take. Good mentorship is a huge consideration for many to stick around with a company long term.

Delegation for leaders can be an incredibly difficult thing to get right. Not enough autonomy for their team will result in disinterest and frustration. Too much autonomy will lead to inconsistent decisions, and decisions lacking big picture context. Knowing when to *do* vs when to *delegate* can be a lifelong balancing act. But getting it right is how a company scales, while fostering ownership and helping career growth of team members. So consequently, early startup leaders should hire for complementary skills, and find people who excel at doing things they don't do well, or things that they shouldn't be focusing on. Leaders should find all stars, take time to give them all the context, and then give them the wheel. They will then have more time to focus on what their company really needs them to do, which is set a direction and a strategy, and manage from afar. And as others are filling all the necessary gaps, and everyone is executing well, things can scale faster than they could have imagined.

Leaders will also need to make unpopular decisions sometimes, and will have to pick the best of several bad options. But most decisions should not be unpopular. In fact, most decisions should feel revelatory, because your actual decisions should be thought through and make a lot of sense, and almost seem obvious in retrospect. Leaders should ask themselves often, *do my decisions make sense*? Is their team executing decisions because they believe in their judgement, or they are just doing what they are told? If the latter more than the former, leaders will need to rethink their decision making. And if they are not even sure if others believe in their judgement, they are not asking enough questions.

Lastly, great leaders have "strong convictions, held weakly". This is a seemingly paradoxical statement, as they need to be fully committed to decisions, while at the same time leaving room that they might be wrong. But in truth, these two statements go hand in hand. Waiting too long for information before making decisions is harmful, especially for decisions that are reversible, or decisions that don't have a massive impact or use a lot of resources. So by definition, great leaders take a lot of calculated risks while ensuring their teams are being efficient. They also guess right a lot, because they are good at critical thinking. But at the same time, they know there is always a chance for error, and are constantly re-evaluating, measuring, and taking time to research and learn and think. In doing this, they ensure that future decisions become more accurate, without sacrificing more time.

Setting Your Mission

Many founders underestimate how important setting a mission is. A company's mission is their north star that guides strategy, product vision, culture, and even morality. A mission is aspirational–something you always aspire to but can never really achieve:

> *"Our company mission is to organize the world's information and make it universally accessible and useful." (Google)*

> *"Facebook's mission is to give people the power to build community and bring the world closer together."*

> *"Tesla's mission is to accelerate the world's transition to sustainable energy."*

Every major initiative and product feature, as well as how you run your company, treat your employees, and engage your community, should always gut check back to your mission. If it doesn't align, you must question why you are doing it. If your employees are unhappy that something you chose to do is against the mission, that is... an amazing thing, and shows how committed your team really is to your aspirations.

Your Vision And Roadmap

Working down from your mission, the next step is your vision. Where are you headed? What is the logical conclusion to what you're building? What is your exit strategy?

"Strategy without tactics is the slowest route to victory. Tactics without strategy is the noise before defeat."

- Sun Tzu

You can plan well, but without execution, go absolutely nowhere. Startups in particular need "doer" leaders, who are willing to roll up their sleeves and do the work. Doing and reacting with no cohesive strategy is mindless, and wasteful of capital and resources. It will also cause your best and brightest to go someplace else.

After you have articulated your long term vision, you will need to build a product roadmap. A roadmap is a prioritized list of features you intend on building over the next 12 months (6 minimum). Your product roadmap shouldn't be whatever buzzwords are trending now. It also shouldn't be reactive to every problem that is happening today. It also shouldn't change priorities every other quarter.

Your roadmap should be rooted in your mission, vision, and company priorities, leading to annual themes or pillars, and lastly resulting in your features. It should be solving problems for the next 12 months and beyond. It should be thought through and cohesive. Roadmaps are hard. But good ones are the difference between success and failure.

The Software Development Lifecycle (Sdlc)

In technology, this is a topic that's quite important to understand, whether you are a product manager or engineer, or even a business team member or non-technical co-founder. Every feature you launch follows the software development lifecycle, and knowing how your products are planned, developed, deployed, and maintained are critically important for your decision making. The framework of the SDLC is generally the same everywhere, but some of the processes that drive different areas *should* vary between companies based on product, team, resources, and other factors. There have been historically two approaches to SDLC: waterfall and agile. Agile, even as the newer approach, became the dominant methodology over time due to its capability to get projects off the ground faster, and generally speeding up the development cycle. There are definitely negatives to agile, and it would be a mistake to completely dismiss some of the virtues of waterfall. There is also an emerging methodology called "continuous delivery (or deployment)", which involves constantly shipping code with no set releases. This has shown to derisk deployments in general and also allow development teams to move faster, and has been adopted by some major technology companies. But for the purposes of this book, we will mostly focus on agile processes.

The software development lifecycle starts with ideation and planning. Typically product managers[12] will be the central orchestrator across the entire SDLC. They will do market and competitive research, user studies, and more to come up with features to build. They are then responsible for writing product requirements and user stories along with acceptance criteria to provide engineering teams instructions on what to build. There are requirement reviews, revisions, but generally everyone tries to solve for getting coding started ASAP. Speed to market, especially at startups, is more important than having every detail spelled out. This is however not an excuse to be lazy with details.

The development part of the lifecycle will typically be split into "sprints" or "iterations", where large projects are broken into components, and engineering teams code and complete components in a predetermined sequence within each sprint, until the project is complete. At the end of a component being built, other engineers may review the code to see if they can spot any issues. Then, a quality assurance team (QA) will test the functionality against the requirements, and report any bugs. After projects pass code review and QA, the feature is prepared for launch, which includes some go-to-market activities, such as marketing activities (press releases, social media posts, newsletters, blogs), internal documentation and training for sales and account management, pricing and business operations updates, and more. Then, after a feature makes it into production, there is maintenance and continuous iterations and improvements, as well as kicking off new projects, and starting the SDLC over and over again for each one.

Velocity is extremely important to keep track of when you're doing sprint planning. Knowing how much coding engineers can get done in one sprint helps you plan better, and provides clearer delivery dates in the future. But be careful to understand what impacts velocity. Usually, it's not engineers messing around and not working hard enough. There are a number of different factors that can impact their work, but a major one is *context switching*. Engineers can get "in the zone" coding hundreds of lines of code, with functions referencing other functions and variables being declared, and to pull them out of the zone would be disaster. This is not like losing your place in a book, and trying to find it again. A better analogy is if you lost your place in a book, and someone took your book and threw it in a deep pit for you to find. Causing engineers to context switch can cause a one hour project to explode into two or three hours. So protect engineers: keep them out of meetings, don't tap them on the shoulder for random questions, and just let them get as many hours of uninterrupted coding as possible. This also means keeping their sprints "clean". If you find that the queue of work is a hodgepodge of features to be developed, bugs to be fixed, and random small tasks here and there, that context switching can slow velocity down dramatically. If there are too many bugs, and too many small tasks, you either need to say "no" more, or start thinking about support teams or specialized engineering teams to deflect some of that work away from core feature development. 80% of sprints working on just product features is a good number to aim for.

After each project, and some teams even do this each sprint, something called a "retrospective" occurs. The team will meet after a project or sprint is complete, and review what went well, what didn't go well, and if some improvements can be made in the future. I personally feel retros after every sprint is mildly overkill, but situations may be different for your organization. Retros after every major project, and also after any major bugs are discovered in production and fixed, are absolutely necessary.

Lastly, you want to ensure you are measuring how well a feature or process is performing after you deploy them, which are sometimes referred to as KPIs (key performance indicators). Some of what you need to measure should have been included as part of the aforementioned acceptance criteria. But you definitely want to measure a broad range of metrics from usage and adoption, repeat visits, engagement and conversion metrics, bounce rates, revenue, efficiency gains, and other things that might be relevant to your specific business or product.

Depending on the size of the company, you may also have:

1. Project managers who coordinate schedules and dependencies, and generally ensure everyone is hitting deadlines and are accountable for their work
2. User experience (UX) designers, who are responsible for in depth user research, user studies, acceptance testing, designs, and more
3. Automation QA engineers, who are responsible for coding testing plans so they can be run automatically

If a company doesn't have these resources, product managers will typically take up the slack, but generally you don't want this going on too long, as it takes the product manager's attention away from their most important job: understanding in depth all the needs and issues of their users.

This is a very high level overview of the SDLC, and it would benefit everyone to do more research on their own to learn more.

Fundraising

There is a lot of information online about fundraising, which can be a complex and stressful process. The technical details of fundraising are out of scope for this book, but I have added a few free online resources below. Some general concepts to understand:

1. **Seed round** is your initial round of funding, sometimes referred to as a "friends and family" round. This can be from tens of thousands of dollars to up to $1-2 million on the very high side.
2. **Series A, Series B, Series C, etc,** are your subsequent rounds, with each round (typically) larger than the previous.
3. **Exit strategy** is your eventual goal, which typically means you are either getting acquired by another company, or going public (IPO). You can also do neither and sustain independently as

a private company, but this is not an "exit".

4. **Venture capital firms** are investment companies that provide funding to startups. Different firms will invest in different stages of a company. For example, larger firms may only invest in Series C or later companies, while smaller firms will invest in seed and Series A.

5. **General partners (GPs)** and a group of investors that run VC firms

6. **Funds** are rounds of funding raised by GPs for their VC firms

7. **Limited partners (LPs)** are individuals who would like to invest their money in startups, but are happy letting these VCs choose the companies for them.

8. **Equity** is a piece of a company in the form of stock, usually expressed as a percentage or in "basis points", and are given to investors in exchange for funding, to employees as part of compensation, and can be given for other purposes, such as compensating advisors.

9. **Carry** is how GPs make money, which is a percentage of the *profits* generated by a fund, usually 20%. They also charge a management fee, usually 2%. You will hear this referred to as "2 and 20".

10.   **Dilution** occurs when you

issue new stock, usually for your next round of funding, which will decrease your existing stockholders' ownership percentage of your company. This is not necessarily a bad thing, as you are usually, but not always, getting a smaller percentage of a much bigger "pie".

11.   **Liquidation preferences** determine who gets money first and under what terms in the case of an exit, and typically, LPs will get the most favorable preferences.

12.   **Incubators** are VCs that specialize in investing in only seed stage companies, but also assist these companies with various things, such as office space and training.

There is much much more to learn, and you really should take the time to learn as much as possible before jumping into shark infested waters. A well known incubator called YCombinator has tried to simplify the funding process with something called SAFEs, which is something early stage startups should be leveraging as much as possible.

Some free and excellent online resources:

1. THE HOLLOWAY GUIDE TO Equity Compensation: https://www.hollo-

way.com/g/equity-compensation
2. A Guide to Seed Fundraising: https://blog.ycombinator.com/how-to-raise-a-seed-round/
3. YC's New Guide to Raising a Series A: https://blog.ycombinator.com/ycs-series-a-guide/
4. SAFE financing documents: https://www.ycombinator.com/documents/
5. Many of the posts on Both Sides of the Table: http://www.bothsidesofthetable.com/
6. You can also keep up with a lot of VC news at: https://pitchbook.com/news

Budgeting

Even if you have raised many millions of dollars, it is still wise to be very frugal with your money. There are a plethora of horror stories of companies running out of cash, unsure how to make payroll next month, and then their surefire next round of funding falls through, and they have to have layoffs, shut down completely, or panic sell their company (if they can even find a buyer) in a very unfavorable position. You will often find yourself with unfavorable deal terms if investors know you're desperate for money. Also, bad things can happen, from lawsuits, natural disasters, employee misconduct, accidents, all of which can cause a sudden and unexpected financial shock. You should use capital wisely, to grow your company aggressively and hire the best people, but set budgets everywhere so you can predict your burn rate, control your costs, and ensure your company's long term health. Additionally, by building a culture of frugality and a scarcity mindset, your team will find ingenious solutions to solve problems instead of just throwing money at it, and this type of mindset can also trigger innovative thinking about your product.

This also implies you need to track your financials properly, as well as ensure you are collecting your revenue effectively. If you don't have a clue how to do corporate finance, don't worry– a lot of founders don't either. There are a wealth of resources available online, as well as templates you can use to track your finances. A great resource for learning the most important financial statements is the SEC's "Beginners' Guide to Financial Statements" online article[13].

There are also many tools available to automate your invoicing and collections. You don't need to pay for an expensive enterprise solution in your early days. And even some of the expensive ones will have "startup pricing", which will be deeply discounted for smaller companies. You will need to evaluate which tools fit your industry and needs at the time, which just takes a bit of (free) online research.

CHAPTER 5:
COMPLEXITY
COST

C omplexity cost is, by definition, introducing long-term, counter-productive complexity in your product or organization by
making short-sighted first order decisions. Complexity cost can be a slow-building poison that
eventually paralyzes your company if you aren't
mindful of it. It can cause the following to happen:

1. Users will be overwhelmed by options
2. Settings and features that start displaying undesired combinatorial effects
3. A product that becomes impossible to
   maintain and diagnose over time
4. Teams and processes unable to scale
5. Business teams keep duct taping over

broken processes instead of making progress
6. Decisions become more short sighted as you're constantly in fire-fighting mode

There are more impacts depending on what you made overly complex, and what your business is doing. But a great example in the market happened back in the late 1990s and early 2000's, Yahoo! was a dominant web presence on the Internet, peaking at 100 million pageviews per day in 1997. Yahoo!'s homepage was a "web portal", where users could access just about anything they needed from a single place: email, news, sports, stocks, maps, games, and much more. It achieved massive product / market fit in those early days of the Internet, where web surfing habits were drastically different than what they are today. Web surfers wanted a home destination, or "launchpad", where they could quickly access all the activities and info they were familiar with once they logged on. And just about every service that Yahoo! was offering objectively delivered value to their users.

The Search Bar

One important feature on Yahoo!'s homepage was their search bar, which would allow you to find websites that matched whatever terms you were searching for. And even though that search bar held prominent placement at the top of the page, it was still quite lost in the sea of overwhelming choice that was shown to users on every visit.

*Yahoo's homepage, circa 1999. Credit: Creative Commons

It was actually quite incredible what you could accomplish from your Yahoo! portal. And Yahoo! would tweak content and layouts over time, improving the experience, and eventually even allowing you to curate your own landing page. But a lot of traffic was still derived from the search bar, and subsequent search results.

Then along came Google. Not only did Google build an extremely powerful search engine to compete against Yahoo!, based on the thesis they could achieve more relevancy by examining the relationships between websites (PageRank), but they also reduced their homepage to really focus on just one single element: their search bar. In the earlier days, a few minimal links would appear, such as tabs to access categories of searches and their shopping product, Froogle, but the major focus of the page was the search bar. Over time, those links disappeared, and the simple and clean homepage with just a search bar has stayed consistent all the way to present day:

*Google's homepage, 2019

But this didn't happen by accident. There was purposeful intent to make the page uncluttered, and to keep it this way over time.

> Google didn't just stumble into its home page design; it didn't arrive at simplicity by default. The company actually developed a rigorous system that imposed tight restrictions upon what could and could not be added to the page. Its leaders had to stand firm against Google's own creative and well-meaning engineers. And in some cases they even

had to defy the wishes of customers.[14]

This design decision achieved several things:

1. Got ahead of changing behaviors: users were now *looking* for things on the Internet, rather than having static content presented to them every day in a portal
2. Focused users on a single core and powerful feature, web search, and reduced any mental overhead of navigating around Google
3. Faster page load times with fewer elements to load (many studies have shown high abandonment rates on pages that are slow to load)
4. And most importantly, low *complexity cost* for Google's users, as well as Google's product and engineering teams

Yahoo's popularity started to wane, eventually leading to the infamous "Peanut Butter Manifesto" in October of 2006, an internal memo written by a Yahoo! executive named Brad Garlinghouse. The manifesto claimed that Yahoo! had lost its focus by trying to build and maintain so many products.

"I've heard our strategy described as spreading peanut butter across the myriad opportunities that continue to evolve in the online

world. The result: a thin layer of investment spread across everything we do and thus we focus on nothing in particular.

I hate peanut butter. We all should."[15]

The manifesto also pointed out a secondary effect of having so many products: Yahoo! now had a highly redundant team that would compete against each other in the same product lines.

We lack a focused, cohesive vision for our company. We want to do everything and be everything–to everyone. We've known this for years, talk about it incessantly, but do nothing to fundamentally address it. We are scared to be left out. We are reactive instead of charting an unwavering course. We are separated into silos that far too frequently don't talk to each other. And when we do talk, it isn't to collaborate on a clearly focused strategy, but rather to argue and fight about ownership, strategies and tactics.

Fast forward to late 2019, and Google holds an 88% market share for search, while Yahoo! holds only 2.8%[16], and Google has a market cap of over $800 billion, while Yahoo!'s market cap is reportedly below $40 billion. There are many factors that caused these two companies' paths to diverge so drastically, but a primary cause of Yahoo!'s fate was the inability to unwind themselves from the complexity in their product and teams that had been building over time.

Leveling In Poker

One of the most fun but challenging strategies in poker is "leveling" your opponents. Essentially, when playing a hand against a particular opponent, you must understand what level of thinking they are capable of, and utilize tactics to exploit their capabilities. At the same time, your opponents are doing the same to you. This can lead to complex one-upmanship as players engage in a battle of wits hand after hand after hand. A great way to observe elite players engage in leveling wars is by watching videos of poker games that are posted online, with commentators calling the play-by-play. Seeing how the best players think through hands and exploit their opponents is both a fun and educational activity, as many players use these streams as coaching tools. Seeing leveling applied in live poker games by the best players will really exemplify why poker is truly a game of skill. The levels of poker thinking are:

- Level 1: What hand do I have?
- Level 2: What hand does my opponent

have?
- Level 3: What does my opponent think I have?
- Level 4: What does my opponent think I think they have?
- Level 5: What does my opponent think I think they think I have?

And this can conceivably keep going, but it is rare that many players will go above level 5, both due to how difficult it is, as well as the very low frequency in which it ever really needs to be applied. But there is a lot you can already do to gain an edge by understanding the first 5 levels of poker.

For example, level 1 thinkers will be pretty hard to bluff. They are only thinking about their own hands, so if you try to represent a hand that is stronger than theirs, they... just won't care. If they have a strong hand, it will be unlikely they will fold. So the correct tactic against level 1 thinkers is to be patient, and play your strong hands aggressively to ensure you maximize profit with your winning hands. You probably don't need to worry much about level 1 thinkers trying to exploit you.

Level 2 thinkers consider the strength or weakness of your hand when playing. When they bet, they are not betting based on just the strength of their hand, but also based on the strength of *your* hand. You must show more care around level 2 thinkers, because this is the first level where exploitation starts coming into play.

Level 2 thinkers will eventually lead some to level 3 thinking. This introduces a new layer of complexity to the game: playing your own "perceived" hand in a way that can exploit your opponent. For example, you're in a situation where your opponent seems to have a hand that can beat yours with more cards to be dealt, and so far, the "community cards" contain two hearts. The next card dealt brings another heart, which doesn't help your hand at all, but now completes a flush if someone holds two hearts in their hand. Although you don't actually have hearts, you can *represent* that you do against an opponent who *perceives* you might have hearts. This can lead to you winning a hand where you didn't have the best holding, which is how poker players win in the long run: winning hands constantly that you aren't supposed to win.

And you can see how this can extend to level 4, level 5, level n thinking: a constant game of one-upmanship while figuring out where your opponent is. And those that can think at level 4, can also decide in a hand to dial it back to lower level if that's the optimal way to exploit an opponent. A player can think they should play a hand based on level 4 thinking, so their opponent may play their hand like level 3, even though they are capable of playing at level 4. However, a more classical way for players to beat themselves with "leveling" is when they overestimate what their opponent is capable of, and apply more complex higher level thinking in situations where it is not appropriate. Applying advanced concepts against the lowest level thinkers will not only be a waste of time, but also *completely the wrong strategy*. Playing straightforward would be the correct strategy most of the time, which is a perfect analogy for keeping things simple when running a startup.

Future Proofing

Overthinking is a common cause of increased complexity cost. Introducing complexity where it is not needed can have disastrous long term consequences, and hurt your ability to make progress in the future. This can apply to your product, your operations when running your team, as well as when you're sitting at the poker table. Coming up with overly complicated solutions to first order problems will raise the effort needed to accomplish a task for very little gain, and sometimes cause more harm than good. There is a science to creating simple and elegant solutions that can solve problems broadly and can "kill two birds with one stone", without causing issues in other parts of the product or organization.

When a product is designed simply, the maintenance and diagnosis of issues will be more efficient, and the rate of overall issues in the long run would likely decrease. When an overly complex thought process is used to arrive at a solution, that solution will also be complex to users when presented to them. Users don't like complexity, and they will find something else to solve their problems if your product keeps getting more complex.

If all this is true, why does complexity still happen? Often, complexity cost is introduced inadvertently with the best intentions. Sometimes, users and business facing teams have a tendency to push *implementation details* to product managers and engineers. Business teams and users may think they are helping their product counterparts, but in fact, they are often doing the opposite. Business teams do not have the big picture and cross-dependency context of how features interact with, and impact, other parts of a product. They may not be able to evaluate engineering effort and risk for different options, or know what all the other priorities are across the organization. Nor do they, or should they, spend all their time thinking through use cases, edge cases, and secondary and tertiary order effects of feature design, which are critical considerations for reducing complexity cost. In fact, giving product teams implementation details will often cause *more* work and time to unravel what the suggestions are trying to solve, and also as those teams try to de-risk any proposed solutions. The most useful information to provide the product teams are actually *business goals*. What problem are you trying to solve? Who are you trying to solve it for? And what do successful outcomes look like after building a solution? Here is an examples for context:

> **Business goal:** *Our sales team wants to distribute leads by geography in our enterprise CRM software.*

> **Implementation detail:** *Our sales team wants to distribute leads via a static list of zip codes which the sales team will maintain.*

You can see how the business goal states user needs and the problem space clearly, and give product and engineering the flexibility to come up with solutions that can balance a number of different factors, such as finding an optimal user experience, adhering to a company style guide, reducing load time, lowering engineering level of effort, or considering future changes in the pipeline. The implementation details on the other hand do not allow for any of those things, and do not allow the product and engineering teams to understand what the true root problems are. To see how complexity cost can appear later: what happens when new sales team members join, and you need to change the allocation of zips? You would need to make a manual change each time, and the engineer will have to make an update each time, which doesn't scale. And if the leads become unevenly distributed based on zips, then you may need to move things around more. And if there is a manual list being maintained somewhere, error rates may be significant. A better idea would be to find a programmatic way that auto distributes based on territories that does not need manual maintenance and distribution. But this is something an engineer can come up with only if you allow them to.

A second cause of complexity cost was actually already discussed in an earlier chapter: not thinking through the secondary and tertiary effects of your decisions. Attempting to fix first order problems in a vacuum without thinking about the future will almost always lead to bad consequences, and will result in your team constantly duct taping things to fix the problems caused by previous decisions. Often under the umbrella of good intentions, a reckless call may have been pushed through because an urgent issue needed to be fixed or a big client demanded a custom feature, and just trying to solve a first order problem quickly seemed like the best choice at the time. But this type of mindset, when taken too far, can lead to disaster. Let's look at another example:

Business goal: *Users of our social media app*

are frustrated with the inability to curate their feeds.

Implementation detail: *Users want to pick exactly who they see content from.*

The implementation detail, if pushed through without taking the time to consider use cases, can definitely add complexity cost down the line. When users in a social media platform pick exactly who they see content from, it can cause them to get through their feeds too quickly, and not visit as often. It will also reduce the network effects of the platform. Then, after giving users this option, it would be hard to take it away, and then you may have to start adding more options to compensate for the second order effects of the original decision, rather than finding a more elegant solution in the first place.

When building products, it's not hard to make a button. So it might be tempting to give users or business teams a button when they ask for one. But each product decision must factor not only short term needs, but the long term health of the product. All the buttons that you ever built, and keep building, can combinatorially start doing unexpected things. Users may start to get overwhelmed with options. Your product will become increasingly too confusing for your users, as well as too complex for your engineering team to maintain or diagnose issues efficiently, and will slow the production of new features to a crawl. If you allow complexity cost to run rampant in your product, you will begin to lose your users, while at the same time making it harder for your team to build better solutions that would help win some of those users back. Engineering teams need to focus on building features instead of constantly fixing issues or paying off technical debt. Complexity cost is also very interrelated with making trade-offs, which will be discussed in the next chapter.

Complexity cost is an important concept to understand in product management, but also broadly applicable to all types of decision making, including when making decisions for your organization. Complexity cost on teams will cause management of day to day tasks to be a needlessly frustrating experience. The end state to complex and short-sighted processes that don't make the proper trade-offs will be a team in constant fire-fighting mode, with no room to plan long term, and resulting in an inability to scale.

The best companies who have leaders that think through things thoroughly may exhibit the following traits:

1. A calm, stoic organization, less people "running with scissors"
2. High alignment and communication

(due to low complexity of things that need to be communicated)

3. Consistent scaling, seeing an ability to do more with less resources and time
4. Less fire-fighting, more room for future planning
5. Clear vision, clear mission, clearly articulated path to forward
6. High trust in leadership

This is the type of organization you want to be working for, and this type of organization will also tend to attract the highest performers. So always consider the cost-benefit of all your decisions, know the upside and downside, the long term impacts, and make sure you are always tracking and seeking to reduce the potential complexity costs of your decisions.

CHAPTER 6: MAKING TRADE-OFFS

U p to this point, we have focused on idea-tion via identifying user needs, prac-ticing good decision making, and being vigilant of complexity cost as we go. We also touched on the software development lifecycle (SDLC) as part of "The Getting Started Checklist" chapter. The foundation we have built should allow you to more confidently set a path forward for your startup, and give your team something structured and tangible to build. User research and feedback are incorporated, as well as hope-fully some novel innovations that others couldn't see. You've built a product roadmap, have de-tailed project priorities and requirements, engin-eering estimates are done, and the team is ready to execute.

Then, it dawns on you: how on earth can you build all of this in a reasonable amount of time? You're still a young startup, not a lot of money in the bank, and have very limited engineers, support teams, and other resources. The roadmap now looks daunting. And as you keep building and building, other parts of the business and product will need resources for maintenance, which will divert some of the resources needed to continue building new features.

Time to cover one of the most important topics in decision making and prioritization: how to make *trade-offs*.

Trade-offs can be defined as taking into account other factors when considering how to move forward with a decision, which *may* ultimately make you take a different route. The different route might be sub-optimal for some first order use cases, but is necessary to account for those other factors, as you must consider both what you *gain*, as well as what you might *lose* with a given decision.

You actually make trade-offs all the time. Cooking at home instead of ordering takeout is a trade-off that factors in cost, time, eating healthy, tracking calories, how tired you are, and some other factors. Reading this book right now instead of a different book, or even watching a movie is a trade-off. Choosing to prioritize a feature that your 10 biggest clients have asked for instead of a feature that the other 500 needs is a trade-off. Choosing to optimize for accuracy instead of speed with a process is also a trade-off. You might argue that every decision that you make is in actuality a trade-off of some sort.

Mixed Strategies In Poker

One poker concept that exemplifies making trade-offs is something called *mixed strategies*. Usually when encountering any given situation at a poker table, you can choose to play a fairly standard way. You may choose to raise or re-raise every time you have a flush draw or a big pair, like AA or KK, for instance. And always fold when you have 42 or 83. The standard way will typically be the *optimal* way, which means by choosing this play, you will maximize your win rate and earnings. For example, we can confidently say that raising or re-raising with AA before the flop is the standard play, and would typically yield the most success, at least in the short term. This seems like a nice solution to a first order problem.

But if you play the same standard way over and over again, you form a pattern that players will begin to adjust to. You start to become predictable, and then soon, you will become exploitable. If you play AA the standard way all the time, when you decide to *not* raise when playing a hand, opponents can be relatively sure you don't have AA. And as players adjust accordingly, you will find yourself winning less money with your strongest hands, and being beaten more frequently with your weaker hands. And as soon as players have adjusted to you, poker becomes very hard, and you will need to figure out how to counteract their adjustments.

So as you run into the same hands and the same situations over time, mixing up your play and doing things differently seems like a good idea. Playing in unpredictable ways will keep your opponents off guard, and make you harder to exploit. This is known as deploying *mixed strategies*. If, for example, you raise or re-raise sometimes with AA, and sometimes don't raise, and you follow the same pattern for a hand like 98, it will make your play "balanced". In any given situation, you can have a *wide range* of different hands, so players cannot make any assumptions about your holdings. For example:

Your opponent raises to $100, and you re-raise to $300 with K♥K♠. Your opponent goes all-in for $3000, and you call. Your opponent has A♠A♣, and you lose after the community cards don't help you in any way.

The same opponent calls for $40. You raise to $120 with J♦J♥. Your opponent calls.

The flop comes T♥8♠2♠, which looks like a safe board for you. Your opponent checks, you bet $120, and your opponent raises to $360. You call. The turn is the 2♦, another safe card. Your opponent bets $500, you call. The river is the 5♥. Your opponent goes all in for $2000. You don't love this situation, as your opponent is indicating he has a hand better than JJ, but you call. Your opponent shows A♦A♥, which is surprising, since he had raised the last time he had AA, like most players would do.

The same opponent / nemesis calls for $40. You raise to $120 with the Q♠Q♣, and he calls. The flop is 8♥7♥3♦. He checks, you bet $120. He raises to $360. Ugh. What does he have? A straight draw, a flush draw? You beat those hands. A8? You beat that too. Seems like a call is warranted here. Except you can no longer rule out AA. Or KK. And he also might have two pair or a set. Now you are quite lost in a hand that should be relatively straightforward, because your nemesis mixed up his play.

You can see how exploiting your play becomes drastically more difficult if you can deploy mixed strategies well. If you can balance your play such that your opponents are constantly unsure how to play against you, you will find it much easier to exploit *them*.

But there is something else to consider, since it's never that easy. By mixing your strategies, you are in effect choosing to play some hands sub-optimally. Not raising with AA can get you into heaps of trouble after the flop, as you may attract multiple players into the pot with you. AA does not fare well when going against a lot of other hands at the same time.

> *An opponent raises to $40, and you just call instead of raising with A♠A♣, and two other opponents call. The flop comes J♣T♠9♥. That's not the best flop, as the board texture is considered "wet", which means there are suited and connected cards, and is very likely your opponents have hit something they would like to continue with, or perhaps play aggressively. The original raiser checks, and you decide to bet $80. Right on cue, the next opponent to act raises to $200. This indicates tremendous strength, as there are still three players left to act behind him, including you, the original bettor. One of the other players calls, and the action is back on you. What a mess.*

But this is a chance you will have to take sometimes to achieve balance, and you can see how you might not be maximizing given situations today. This can cause you to win less money in the short term, or even outright lose a hand that you should have won. But the *trade-off* you are making is for future plays, as you believe that you will maximize your win rate over time, by keeping your opponents off-guard.

However, we should keep in mind from our previous lesson on complexity cost: going too far just trying to be tricky all the time could become confusing, and you might play so many hands poorly in the short term that any gains you get in the long term would be offset. This would overall hurt your win rate, so you must choose wisely when to deploy mixed strategies. The lesson to learn here is that when making trade-offs, decisiveness and simplicity are still important considerations in decision making. Despite all that, erring on the side of focusing on the long view will more often than not will be the optimal play in both poker and running a startup. The exceptions are when you have to correct an urgent disaster to "keep the lights on", but with good long term planning and strategy, and diligent budgeting, you should hopefully be able to keep these instances to a minimum.

Opportunity Cost

When making business decisions and building products with complexity, long timelines, and non-guaranteed outcomes, your ability to make trade-offs becomes as important as your ability to actually ideate and build the product. Trade-offs will allow you to move faster, stay lean with your decision making, and, with some evaluation, learn how to "future-proof" your choices. Future-proofing will require an evaluation post-mortem on the choices you had made. One specific area to focus the evaluation on is your *opportunity costs*.

Opportunity costs can be described as imagining what you *could* have done instead with the resources you had available, if you hadn't gone forward with your "first" choice. If you had one engineer work on a login page for your site for one week, what could that engineer have done instead in that one week? Build a profile page? Scale the backend to handle traffic increases? Put additional monitoring in place to catch issues faster? If you had gone forward with the login page, would any of those choices been better for your users and for the business? If not, how can we learn from this so we can choose better the next time? Going through this exercise allows you to understand the consequences of your decisions, and also helps you see priorities better. It could be as simple as choosing to remodel your kitchen instead of your bathroom, or it could be as impactful as choosing to focus your business on video stores instead of video streaming. Each decision you make will have a cost, but also a benefit. That cost could also do a lot of other things, so how do we maximize our benefits?

Back in 1997, Eric Yuan was one of the first engineers at Webex, a video-conferencing company in Milpitas, California. Webex would go public in 2000, and eventually be acquired by Cisco for $3.2 billion in 2007. By 2010, Yuan had helped grow the team from 10 engineers to more than 800, and contributed to revenue growth from $0 to more than $800 million.[17] But Yuan was unhappy, and expressed:

> *The service simply wasn't very good. Each time users logged on to a Webex conference, the company's systems would have to identify which version of the product (iPhone, Android, PC or Mac) to run, which slowed things down. Too many people on the line would strain the connection, leading to choppy audio and video. And the service lacked modern features like screen-sharing for mobile.[18]*

He pestered his bosses for a year to rebuild Webex, but was not given the support to do so. Frustrated with the constraints of a big company, and convinced of his idea to build a better, more user friendly video-conferencing solution, Yuan left Cisco and founded Zoom. Zoom didn't really provide a dramatic innovation in video-conferencing, but it did do solve many user problems better, and with better technology:

1. It was a blazing fast, lightweight Web app
2. It identified the type of device a user was using so you didn't need different versions
3. It protected from updates on Chrome, Firefox or Safari that might have introduced bugs
4. It could still function when the connection was bad, up to a 40% data loss
5. It also undercut its rivals in price

You will often see this same pattern with the most successful companies: an intense focus on user needs which borders on obsession. Yuan and his team clearly understood video conferencing users, and they were willing and able to make things better in ways that other solutions did not. Zoom went public in 2019 at a $9 billion valuation. Later in 2020, while the world was unexpectedly hit by the Coronavirus and swarms of tech workers started to work from home, Zoom's valuation exploded as the software skyrocketed in popularity, and continued to handle the surge of usage with no apparent service disruptions.

But back at the decision point where Yuan was debating leaving Cisco, his wife had questioned his decision to give up such a lucrative and secure job in Silicon Valley. The couple was also concerned about how much time Yuan would be able to spend with his family, which included three young children. Yuan had a decision here, and the opportunity cost was *his own time*. He could either stay and continue trying to convince Cisco executives to allow him to rebuild a poor product, or he could leave and pursue his vision. So what could he have been considering? Certainly on one hand was high compensation, big company benefits, and stability for his family. On the other side was uncertainty, but a vision that could pay off in the long run, if Yuan, and his wife and children, were willing to sacrifice time and money in the short term. An additional benefit to going off on his own was being his own boss, and being able to build the product he wanted without obstruction. Personal utility and happiness is also an important factor, which sometimes gets lost in the hard economics.

So the opportunity cost would be potentially the next decade of his life, as that is the typical timeline a startup needs to reach something as big as an IPO. But startups also fail at a 90% clip, which lowers the expected value of what a good outcome might be, as there is always a high risk of failure. This was a tough decision, as it is for almost everyone who enters the startup world in this way. Ultimately, Yuan certainly made the right call on the opportunity cost of how we should spend the next eight years of his life, as Zoom has impacted society for the better, and Yuan is a newly minted billionaire.

♠ ♠ ♠

But an important note on trade-offs and opportunity costs: don't suffer from analysis paralysis. It is easy to get lost in all the potential options and paths you can take, and to overthink and introduce needless complexity into your own thought process and decisions. It is also easy to second guess yourself constantly. In actuality, second guessing is a healthy attribute of competent people, which was shown in a study of the cognitive bias known as the "Dunning-Kruger Effect":

The competent students underestimated their class rank, and the incompetent students overestimated theirs, but the incompetent students did not estimate their class rank as higher than the ranks estimated by the competent group...

...Moreover, competent students tended to underestimate their own competence, because they erroneously presumed that tasks

easy for them to perform were also easy for other people to perform.[19]

But second guessing can definitely go too far when evaluating trade-offs and opportunity costs. We learned earlier how to make "80%" decisions to ensure we were being decisive and execution oriented. Don't lose sight of that, even when making trade-offs. All the concepts in this book are meant to be used together for best results, combined into a powerful mindset that can be deployed across a broad range of problems and initiatives.

A Trade-Off Exercise

An exercise will be helpful to drive home the importance of trade-offs. WiFi cameras are an important security device for the home, and for businesses. It allows you to stream and record indoor and outdoor video, with a wide range of notification and detection options. Back in the early days of Internet security cameras, you couldn't just go home, flip out your phone, and connect your camera to your WiFi with a few clicks. You needed to log into your router, and configure all these settings to connect the camera, which was intimidatingly technical for the average person, as well as just a pain in the ass. So today's WiFi cameras bring you security as well as ease-of-use, as everything can be set up and monitored on your phone fairly simply.

So let's say you're trying to build a WiFi camera that:

1. Records and stores video
2. Detects motion
3. Uses artificial intelligence to recognize if motion is a threat
4. Sounds an alarm if it recognizes a threat
5. Notifies you based on your preferences
6. Allows you to press a button on a notification to call 911

Let's assume all these features are priorities for your launch, and let's say the initial estimate from engineering is ten months. There is a competitor in the market already with some of these features already. You know of another competitor who is close to getting to market, but you're not sure what features they are coming with. And then you get an unpleasant surprise, the AI was underestimated, and additional two months are needed to complete everything. Can you wait a year to get this product out? Your competitors would like that, I'm sure.

So let's see if there are some things we can do to reduce scope to get this product out faster, while still delivering a good solution to our users. Earlier, we talked conceptually about "scoring" features for certain factors or attributes, so let's try that here:

Feature	Revenue impact	Risk	Level of effort	Product fit	Innovation	Score
Record and store video	5	-1	-2	5	1	8
Detect motion	5	-2	-2	5	2	8
AI threat detection	4	-4	-4	3	5	3
Threat alarm	3	-5	-3	3	5	4
Notifications	5	-1	-3	5	1	7
911 button	2	-5	-2	2	2	-1

Depending on a variety of factors, such as short term company goals, mission alignment, availability of resources, competitive landscape, and more, you can *weight* certain factors by applying a multiplier or even simply adding a +1 or -1. For example, you may weight revenue impact and innovation higher in a year where you're willing to differentiate and grab market share at high cost. Or you can weight product fit and risk if your team is lean, and you're trying to still find product / market fit. But for simplicity, let's assume no weighting was done, like in the above table. It seems that two features clearly stand out as needed for launch: detect motion and notifications. One feature looks like it can be scratched, at least for your first version: the 911 button.

Of the two borderline features, the threat alarm and AI threat detection, they are both high risk, but are also coupled together in terms of functionality: the threat alarm is dependent on threat detection to be in place before it can work. Threat detection might be useful on its own, and the owner can still get notifications on their phone or other devices. So maybe it's a good idea to scratch threat alarm from v1, because if something goes wrong with threat detection, it will impact the building of the threat alarm. And there does seem to be a reasonable workaround with notifications.

So let's take a look at the revised scope for v1:

1. Record and store video
2. Detects motion
3. Uses artificial intelligence to recognize if motion is a threat
4. Notifies you based on your preferences

We lost two pretty big features, but we traded them off for what can be a much faster product to market. So does this look like a product that users would still love? It does "table stakes" for a WiFi camera, such as recording video and sending notifications. It detects motion, which is an important feature. It has a big innovation, which we kept in scope: threat detection with AI. It looks like we cut a little over 30% of the scope based on level of effort, so it looks like we can get something done in eight months instead of twelve. That seems like a pretty good trade-off for something that should still hit product / market fit well.

That kind of velocity gain is huge for momentum and morale, and allows your sales and marketing teams to get out there sooner and start fighting for market share with a tangible product. You can also iterate to your next version more quickly, as users will start using the product and providing feedback. More importantly, they may start using these cameras for things you never thought of, which could inform you on how to improve your product more efficiently. Taking a year to get to this point could have led to bad outcomes, from ceding more market share to competitors, to user behavior potentially changing direction away from your solutions (ie "best laid plans"). Lastly, you can survey your users first to gauge interest in your AI feature, and they will give more informed responses now that they know what the overall product looks and feels like. This looks like good decisioning overall in making the correct trade-offs to get a usable product out faster.

CHAPTER 7: DON'T BE OUTCOME ORIENTED

While poker is primarily a game of skill, there is still a high degree of luck, especially in the short term. A single poker tournament with a lot of players is very difficult to win. It's not as bad as playing the lottery, but the odds are definitely stacked against you, even if you are a very good professional. Typically, only 15-20% of the field will make any money in a tournament, and most of the money is concentrated in the top few spots, with the lion's share going to first place. To even "cash" in a tournament (i.e. make any money), you need to dance around a field of landmines, from bad short term

111

variance, to sometimes very tough pros, to unpre-dictable amateurs that can be quite difficult to play against.

But we are learning to focus on the long term, not the short term. We don't worry about the outcome of a decision today, but rather consider what would happen if I were to make this decision 1000 times? Would I get good outcomes 90%? 10%? 50%? And if you play 1000 poker tourna-ments and only expect to make money less than 10% of the time, what strategies and frameworks can we execute to make that percentage higher?

The World Series Of Poker

To give some context on the difficulty of poker tournaments, the 2019 World Series of Poker main event, the biggest tournament of the year worldwide, paid $10 million to first place, $800,000 to 10th place, and $15,000 for players who finished between 1063rd and 1286th place. 6,420 players total played the tournament, which meant 5,357 players made no money at all. Here were the official top 10 payouts, to indicate how "top heavy" tournaments are:

1. $10,000,000
2. $6,000,000
3. $4,000,000
4. $3,000,000
5. $2,200,000

6. $1,850,000
7. $1,525,000
8. $1,250,000
9. $1,000,000
    10. $ 800,000

But on any given day, with so many different types of players playing, really anyone can win a poker tournament, even a novice against the best players in the world. In fact, amatuer players often make the final table of the WSOP main event, and some actually win, changing their lives forever. But just because a player wins, whether they are an amatuer or a pro, it does not mean they didn't make any mistakes, or that they clearly played better than everyone else. If you followed the winner and watched every hand they played throughout a tournament (and the main event lasts for over a week), you would most certainly find multiple instances of poorly played hands and lucky situations. The best pros would admit the same thing, and are often their own harshest critic.

Players who find success while playing poorly in the short term, would be making a big mistake to think they can continue to play the same way and still see success in the long run. Going back to the first chapter, seeing the odds of 72 against AK (32%) gives you some idea of how this is possible. You can call 72 winning "getting lucky", but in actuality, it's just winning the percentage it's supposed to win, which is 32%. You can use 72 as an analogy for playing poorly–you can still win a decent percentage of the time in the short run. But in the long run, better play will begin to take over the win rates. This is why over time, the best players will win more often and more consistently. There is a term for the difference between the outcome expected over the long term and the results seen in the short term: variance.

Variance can wreak havoc over your poker results, sometimes for an uncomfortably long time. This can affect a poker player's mental state, and cause them to overreact to situations that were out of their control. For example, players may end up playing their strongest hands less aggressively just because they lost a bunch of times in the past month. This is a huge mistake, because they will not be realizing their maximum expectation from those hands by being gun shy. By continuing to get your money into pots with the best hands, over time, your results will begin to show consistent success. On the other side, if you are playing poorly and getting a lot of money into pots without the best hands, but landing on the "luckier" side of your probabilities, you need to get back to the drawing board and figure out how to play hands more optimally, or else your expectation getting realized means you will be ruined. And as we saw in an earlier chapter on the *Dunning-Kruger Effect*, it is those least competent who will also be the least likely to self-evaluate and continuously seek to improve. So follow the best at their craft instead, who question everything and are constantly trying to learn and get better.

This is why it's important to take this mindset with you everywhere, especially when running a startup. It is critical to take a long term view with your decisions and strategy, and don't over-optimize for short term results, which can be noisy, and thus, often misleading. There is so much variance and external factors that can impact events at startups that it's extremely important to stay focused. On the other side, be brutally honest about your decision making–are you following the framework on critical thinking, considering future consequences, and measurement? The decision is more important than the result, so that's what we should be optimizing for.

The Process And Outcome Matrix

In startups, you can now see how you can sometimes land on the "lucky" side of variance, and achieve a good outcome with a bad process or bad decision. On the other side, you sometimes get bad outcomes from good processes and good decisions, even for long stretches that will test your resolve. If you want to succeed, it is critical you are able to understand the difference, and maintain the discipline to keep making the right decisions. This means you must take the time to evaluate what is actually happening. So how can we do this in practice?

	Good outcome	Bad outcome
Good process	Healthy and self-reinforcing behavior	Recognize you got unlucky, and keep trying
Bad process	Dangerous. Do not mistake this for a repeatable result	I don't know what I expected

This process and outcome matrix draws a good visual framework on how to evaluate your decisions and outcomes. The green boxes in the upper quadrants represent good things you want to repeat, over and over again. The red boxes in the lower quadrants represent things you need to stop doing ASAP, no matter the outcome.

1. Good process, good outcome: well thought through decision making leading to good outcomes is healthy and self-reinforcing, and easy to repeat
2. Good process, bad outcome: check if your decision making is logical and makes sense, and use discipline to keep

grinding away despite the short term variance

3. Bad process, good outcome: this is the most dangerous quadrant, and needs diligent evaluation and blunt honesty to correct, as good outcomes are addicting

4. Bad process, bad outcome: this should be pretty easy to stop, but a good learning opportunity to ensure you recognize what a bad decision looks like

What might be an example of a good process leading to a good outcome? You observe your engineering team is moving very slowly with feature development. They tell you that the part of the system they often work on needs to be "refactored", which means updating the code in an underlying component without changing its core functionality, but delivering improvements in some way. The refactor may take several weeks, but could speed up feature development in the future. So you make a trade-off and prioritize the refactor over feature development, resulting in much faster coding in just a few weeks. Forecasting out 12 months, it looks like the short term sacrifice may result in two additional features being completed, which would not have been possible before. Seems like a very good outcome, with good incentives to keep repeating what you're doing.

What about a good process leading to a bad outcome? We can take that previous example again. After the developers refactored the code, the next project took just as long. It might be a natural reaction to claim that the refactor didn't work, and thus it was a bad decision and trade-off. But upon examination, there were other factors affecting the velocity of those subsequent sprints, unrelated to the refactor. Without changing anything, the following projects indeed exhibited more speed, and it was best that no one was too reactionary to a short term outcome. It also provides some confidence in making similar decisions in the future. Good processes leading to bad outcomes may discourage you from trying again. No one wants to keep facing bad outcomes. But you have to grit your teeth and keep going. Discipline in repeating good processes will show compounding, long term benefits.

What about a bad process leading to a good outcome? Let's keep going with the same example. You decide to *not* let the developers do the refactor, as deadlines are tight, and you can't stop core feature development for several weeks to work on something else. Sometimes, you will have to make tough trade-offs like this. So the developers keep going, and magically with no refactor, hit their deadline on the next project even sooner than expected. Seems easy to scoff at the refactor as a potential huge waste of time, as the developers seemed to have moved even *faster*. But you must examine other factors before drawing a conclusion like that with limited data. In actuality, the developers found a fantastic workaround that delivered the same functionality with half the complexity and in half the time. This had nothing to do whatsoever with the refactor, and is not repeatable for future projects. As a matter of fact, the current project might have finished even faster if the refactor were done first. Be careful drawing conclusions on temporary good outcomes. Bad processes leading to good outcomes is the worst quadrant. These outcomes will strongly encourage you to continue to execute bad decisions. This will lead to disaster in the long term if you don't correct this behavior. Bad processes and decisions leading to good outcomes is really the core issue with being results oriented: being incentivized into making bad decisions that you keep chasing over and over again.

Lastly, what about a bad process leading to a bad outcome? Let's hammer that example one last time. You decide to ask the engineers to do the refactor and work on the feature *at the same time*, and you push for this over their protests. This decision would completely ignore what we have learned so far about context switching and decisiveness. Engineers working on these two tasks concurrently would grind velocity to a halt, as well as frustrate the overall team via lack of leadership on making one call or the other. This unsurprisingly leads to the project even more delayed than if you had just chosen to do the refactor first. You are also now left with a team of frustrated engineers who have lost confidence in you. This type of immediate negative reinforcement should be a healthy slap on the wrist to get back in the lab.

So let's take a look at the quadrants again. The top green quadrants represent processes and decisions that you should keep repeating. Of course, this does not absolve you of continuing to evaluate your decision making, as something that might look like a good decision might end up being the opposite upon further analysis. The bottom red quadrants are processes and decisions that you must stop doing immediately, while also ensuring re-evaluations over time to add confidence to decision making. Nowhere are we really too focused on outcomes, or at least not the short term ones.

An additional benefit to not being results oriented is that it improves your resilience. Bad outcomes won't affect you as much if you are focused on making correct decisions. You will recognize what is bad luck or short term variance, and be able to brush yourself off and keep going. This will also lead to healthy, long term thinking over obsessing over short term and temporary events. We will cover resilience in more detail in a later chapter.

Persistence And Angry Birds

Being persistent is a key attribute of successful startups. But it matters a lot what you are being persistent with. If you persist in bad habits by making bad decisions over and over again, failure will catch up to you eventually. Poisonous complexity and debt will start to pile up, and your progress will be thrashed by constant fire-fighting. Persisting in bad habits is summarized quite eloquently by this quote:

> *The definition of insanity is doing the same thing over and over again, but expecting different results.*

> *- Albert Einstein*

So clearly, staying persistent with good decisions and processes, regardless of outcome, is the proper habit to form. We will get into a list of do's and don'ts for staying persistent at the end of this chapter. But first, let's take a look at a real life example of a startup that exhibited remarkable persistence before eventually achieving massive success: Rovio, the maker of the hit mobile game, Angry Birds. By July of 2013, the game had been downloaded over 3 billion times, making it the most downloaded freemium game ever at the time.[20]

But Rovio took quite a long path to get there, having made *51* games before eventually hitting the jackpot. Back in 2009, six years after they were founded, the company was close to bankruptcy and had to lay off employees, reducing headcount from a peak of 50 all the way down to 12.[21] And they saw the intimidating task in front of them–the extreme risk of building a game of their own original intellectual property, and trying to get mass adoption. They estimated that it would take 10-15 *more* games before one of them would actually hit. And they had just downsized and were in a shaky financial position.

But that 52nd game did hit. It was Angry Birds. The founders at Rovio never gave up, even after building *51* games and only seeing near-bankruptcy as their outcome. But they believed in their ability to build great games, and more importantly, to understand their users. If there is one repeatable process you can be diligently persistent with, it's to truly understand your users, and think through what solutions would delight them, even if your users end up being "everyone". From the same Wired article:

> So we decided we needed to conquer the App Store: but how do we do that?" The Heds did their homework. "We tried to profile the iPhone user and it turned out that it was everybody," says Mikael. So their game would be for everybody, unlike the more niche sci-fi and horror titles that they had previously produced. Rovio came up with other criteria:

the title had to be expandable to other platforms, but work as a pure iPhone game; it should be physics-based (popular on Flash websites at the time); there should be no tutorial; loading times should be minimal, so that you could play happily for just one minute; and it needed an icon which would stand out in the App store...

...Rovio realised that the old rules of distribution -- put a disk in a box, charge £50 for it and leave it there -- didn't apply. The company created an active, continuous relationship with the customer. It offered regular updates for nothing, to keep people playing and talking about the product: "Our game is a great way to communicate with the customer," Mikael says. The team resolved to answer every tweet and fan letter that came in. They incorporated levels designed by fans and discussed their ideas for new birds (among the suggestions: a phoenix bird that ignites the structure). "People felt that here's a gaming company that actually cares."

Rovio stayed persistent with several things: their core idea, building great games for mobile consumers, understanding their users in depth, and being extremely customer centric. They did not waver from this persistence, even in the darkest parts of their timeline, and eventually, that process driven persistence paid off, in a big way.

So which processes do we want to repeat, and ensure we stay persistent with when running startups?

1. Good decisions and processes while not being misled by short term outcomes
2. Really understanding users, and focusing on their needs
3. Making 80% decisions and being action oriented
4. Thinking through trade-offs and opportunity costs
5. Thinking through secondary and tertiary effects of decisions
6. Not introducing complexity cost, and seeking to reduce it over time
7. A scarcity mindset with spending and budgets
8. Caring for the well being and career growth of your team, and seeking to find them mentorship

Which things do we not want to repeat over and over again at startups?

1. Bad decisions and bad processes, combined with chasing short term outcomes
2. Reacting to small sample sizes or fleet-

ing trends
3. Not thinking through decisions, and introducing more problems than you're solving
4. Taking too long to make decisions trying to find 100% of the information
5. Short term thinking with lack of big picture context

What does persistence look like? And how can we make it easier for our teams to practice? We have learned to focus on long term strategy and vision, and if we have done that correctly, the vision should be fairly static. Having a consistent end goal that everyone can aim for will foster persistence. We will say fewer things more often—and if the biggest complaint is that we repeat ourselves, take that as a compliment. In execution, we will seek to repeat processes that make sense, and when good outcomes repeatedly follow, it will be self-reinforcing behavior to start persistent. And in the face of short term failures, our ability to focus on processes instead of outcomes will also promote persistence, as well as another critically important attribute of successful startups: resiliency.

CHAPTER 8:
BEING RESILIENT

R esiliency is your ability to bounce back from failures and setbacks. There are very few vocations that will knock you down more often than poker and startups. But the volume in which you experience setbacks in poker for events completely out of your control can be overwhelming. Over time, the players with staying power can take these setbacks without blinking. You might think these players are just dead inside... and you might be right. But they have trained themselves not to focus on outcomes or short term results, like we learned in the last chapter. If you are really bought into this mindset, reacting to short term setbacks really isn't necessary. And if you can train yourself to be more stoic even when disaster strikes, and view the world objectively and calmly, your ability to stay persistent will improve as a result.

Resilience is even celebrated in one of the most famous poker movies ever made: *Rounders*. There is a great quote from John Malcovich, who plays Teddy KGB, a Russian mobster who is also an excellent poker player, and the chief pro- tagonist of the main character Mike McDermott, played by Matt Damon. In one of their high stakes poker games, where McDermott was able to keep pressing forward in a tightly contested heads up match, Teddy KGB said, "Hanging around, hang- ing around. Kid's got alligator blood. Can't get rid of him". Resiliency is an important trait that is highly respected, even from enemies and com- petitors. Poker players with alligator blood can weather a lot of downswings and keep playing disciplined. Eventually, these disciplined players will recover and continue to thrive. Those that lose their discipline because they are unable to stay persistent, can bury themselves even further, and vastly increase their risk of ruin.

Having a mindset of calm and stoicism even when the world is crashing down around you is a crucial attribute of the best leaders. A leader's job is to turn chaos into structure for their teams, and remove unnecessary overhead so everyone can focus on problems and solutions. Being able to ex- hibit calm during the storm can reassure teams, and help them bridge the gap in times of tem- porary failure. And building that strong culture of resilience will carry companies through a wide range of events, even severe disasters.

The Resiliency Of Airbnb

Back in 2007, Brian Chesky and Joe Gebbia were having trouble making their rent in San Francisco. During a design conference, they noticed that all the hotel rooms in the city were booked, so they came up with the idea to allow guests to pay to stay in their apartment and sleep on air mattresses. This led to the idea that other people might be willing to allow guests to stay in their homes too. This was how Airbnb was born.

The idea never really took off for the first few years, and at one point they were selling Obama and McCain branded breakfast cereal during the 2008 election to fund their company. Chesky's mother asked, "'So wait, are you a cereal company now?", which was a fair question at the time, as they had made more revenue from cereal than they had made from bookings. This fact coupled with their lack of traction certainly cast doubt in the mind of the founders about the legitimacy of their idea.

Airbnb was unable to get those all-important network effects required for a marketplace, simply because the idea was insane to most people–no one wanted to be the first to start allowing guests into their homes.

Everyone thought that they were completely crazy; no one thought this was a good idea. People said to them, "I hope you have another idea. I hope this isn't the only thing you're working on." Or, "People actually do this? What's wrong with them?".

Investors wouldn't even meet with them, or if they did, they just said, "You guys are crazy. There's going to be a murder in one of these houses. There's going to be blood on your hands. I am not touching this with a 10-foot pole." And no one did. They almost didn't get off the ground. They almost had to close up shop because people thought it was that crazy.[22]

There were so many setbacks and rejections along the way. Brian Chesky talked about waking up in the middle of the night with his heart racing, questioning what they were doing. An investor literally got up and left in the middle of a pitch at a coffee shop.

Eventually, they were pushed into applying to the incubator YCombinator by their advisor, Michael Seibel, who was the CEO of Justin.tv at the time. Paul Graham from YCombinator, when pitched the idea of Airbnb, said "People are actually doing this? Why? What's wrong with them?".[23] The pitch was not off to a good start. But at the end of the pitch, Gebbia pulled out a box of cereal and gave it to Graham, explaining that they had sold cereal to keep the company alive. This triggered a different response from Graham: ""Wow, you guys are like cockroaches. You just won't die." One of the best investors and startup thinkers in the world understood the importance of resilience in founders, even more so than their idea. Another clear signal indicating the importance of resiliency, is when VCs pour billions of dollars into investors who exhibit this trait.

Airbnb did get accepted to YCombinator, and Graham would later say to Chesky: "If you can convince people to pay forty dollars for a four-dollar box of cereal, you can probably convince people to sleep in other people's airbeds. Maybe you can do it." Very often, investors bet on founders simply because they think they will eventually figure it out. And those best suited for lasting long enough to figure it out are those with high resiliency and grit.

The Airbnb founders never gave up on their idea, even when it seemed the entire world thought it was terrible. There is another lesson to take away here. Resilience is not just about bouncing back from setbacks and maintaining forward progress. It also means staying steadfast about your vision, even when others don't believe you, or perhaps even ridicule you.

I believe you have to be willing to be misunderstood if you're going to innovate.

- Jeff Bezos

By not giving up on their idea, and not wavering from their vision for the future of hospitality, they were able to weather all the ups and downs, and put themselves into a position where they would eventually succeed. This is an important point to understand when faced with adversity constantly, which is an expectation when building startups and playing poker: survival can always buy you more time until you catch your opportunity. So what was the outcome for Airbnb from the founders' long running patience and resilience? The company was estimated to be worth $4.3 billion in 2019. Not too bad for an idea that people thought was crazy.

A Chip And A Chair

There is even a term for the simple act of survival in poker tournaments: *a chip and a chair*. NLHE tournament poker is an incredibly complex game. It's not simply about trying to win as many hands as possible–it's about trying to survive and accumulate all the chips by the end of the tournament. There are situations where you may take a sub-optimal action because the value of holding on to chips at a certain stage of the tournament is more important than taking a risk to get more. There are other times where you just need to take a risk with all your chips that you wouldn't take otherwise, because as time goes on, your chip stack relative to the blinds (forced bets on every hand) gets shorter, and you must make a few plays to grow your stack so you can survive. In poker tournaments, players are constantly making these trade-offs to maximize their probability to win, and those that execute these strategies well show consistent win rates year after year.

The term *chip and a chair* was made famous during the 1982 World Series of Poker main event by a player named Jack Straus. Jack thought he had been eliminated from the tournament, but actually still had a single chip remaining, hidden under a napkin. He was able to run it up from this single chip, and eventually won the tournament. So the saying goes: all you need is a chip and a chair, and you can still win the tournament. A more recent example was the 2012 WSOP main event winner, Greg Merson. As told by Card Player:

> *Greg Merson shouldn't even be here. The 25-year-old professional poker player was left with just a couple of blinds with 150 players remaining on day 5 after doubling up Fabrizio Gonzalez.*

Merson got it all in with second pair and the nut flush draw, only to lose to Gonzalez and his set. After the stacks were counted down, it was determined that Merson had Gonzalez covered, albeit slightly.[24]

Incredibly, Greg Merson would actually take his handful of chips, stay focused, and then go on to win the entire tournament, taking down a first place prize of $8,531,853. In both stories, the players did not give up after being put into a precarious situation, and were massively rewarded for their patience and persistence.

While these anecdotes make for great stories, the concept of *a chip and chair* is actually thoroughly embedded into poker tournament strategy. Once you're out of chips, you're out of the tournament. Thus, the player who can accumulate all the chips by the end is the winner. But there is a specific strategy that you play when you become the short stack, which means your chip count is running low and you're in danger of being knocked out of the tournament.

Push / fold chart from 888poker

When you are a short stack, you are in a tricky position. You must survive to get a chance to win the tournament, but each round that you play dwindles your stack down further. So you are under a lot of adversity, especially with other players trying to knock you out to increase their chances of winning the tournament by taking your chips. The strategy you must deploy is to play *fewer* hands, and fold a lot of speculative hands that you might normally play. If you play too many speculative hands, you may waste away chips, so that when you eventually get all your money in, you are not maximizing the amount you can win to survive. You must be patient and wait for moderately premium hands before committing your money. The above chart specifies the weakest hand you should commit your money with based on your specific chip stack.

For example, the chart says to only go all in with the hand 22 if you have 15 "big blinds" or less. This means that if the forced bets on each hand are 1000 / 2000, where 1000 is the small blind, and 2000 is the big blind, if your stack is 15,000, that means you have 15 "big blinds". You should not go all in and commit the rest of your chips with 22 if you have greater than 15 big blinds, nor should you commit your money with Q7 if you have 15 bb or more. There are also other situational considerations you need to take on top of the chart, such as how many people are left to act behind you, how close you are to the money, and even how tough the field is relative to your own skill set. These charts are built over thousands and thousands of simulations, and attempt to maximize your win rates in a range of different scenarios. While there are many versions of push / fold charts, the charts themselves just add mathematics to this concept: when you are under adversity in a poker tournament, be patient and resilient, and wait for a good opportunity to commit your tournament life for a shot to keep going. This is exactly what startups need to do when under a lot of adversity. When the odds seem stacked against you, do what you need to survive, such as selling breakfast cereal when trying to build a home rental marketplace. If you can survive for long enough, an opportunity will eventually reveal itself for you to capitalize on.

This is not to say however that a state of adversity is somehow desired. This mindset and context just teaches you how to respond and overcome these inevitable situations in the startup world. But your default should be building great products for your users, and scaling your business after you achieve product / market fit. If you are following a good framework of user focus and good decision making, times of good, healthy progress should hopefully outnumber times of adversity.

The Startup Curve

We now know from observing so many startups that began from nothing and eventually became success stories, is that the path to success is rarely linear, and that failure is part of the journey. Failure is also how you learn to be resilient, just like poker players who find themselves on the wrong side of variance. Failure will also allow you to learn from your mistakes, which is also how you can improve, and set yourself up for a better chance to succeed. The most important point is– failure is *expected*.

A famous image from Paul Graham called the

"startup curve", shows the erratic path of successes and failures that typical startups take:

the startup curve

Credit: Paul Graham via https://andrewchen.co/after-the-techcrunch-bump-life-in-the-trough-of-sorrow/

Startups are never a straight line. Almost all startups go through something like this. When you think things are finally going smoothly, some disaster will inevitably arise. When you seem to be deep in the depths of failure, a surprise success will get you back on the right track. Rinse, lather, repeat.

To get through this, you need a culture of survivorship and resilience. This is why grit is such an important attribute to look for, and to train, in team members. "Grit" has become a broad term in the startup community, finding its way into culture lists and vision statements. But grit isn't just "working harder", or "hustle". Grit is your willingness to stay with problems for longer, and ability to commit more time and energy to solutions, even when the first few times didn't work out. Being fastidious in problem solving will allow you to weather the troughs of startup life, and will set you up to capture the inevitable successes that will come from your hard work. A culture of not sticking to problems will inevitably sink your company as everyone keeps giving up, and half baked solutions riddle the organization.

A team with high grit may encounter a problem and keep attacking it until they find a solution. If other competitors gave up because it was too hard, the gritty team has a high probability of building a *moat*, which means they have built a differentiated product that achieves product / market fit, giving that company an unfair advantage with a solution that others could not build. Thomas Edison famously went through 10,000 prototypes before inventing the light bulb. Innovations and big ideas need grit and resilience to achieve them. And startups who go through the ups and downs of the startup curve need grit and resilience to survive.

However, there is a caveat: sticking to *any* problem might indicate high grit, but may also indicate lack of critical thinking and judgement. Identifying which problems are high priority is as important as having grit to solve those problems.

The inability to separate critical tasks from ones that don't matter will cause you to prioritize the wrong things, and deploy your resources inefficiently. This can be death for a startup, which is always strapped for resources in one way or another. Judicious and careful deployment of resources and decision making year after year is how a startup can scale. Metrics like revenue per employee should be steadily increasing as you continue to make good decisions and focus on the right problems. Pushing problems that don't matter into priority lists will point those metrics in the wrong direction, eventually leading to failure. Another effect will be the demoralization of the team, as they will distrust decisions from the decision makers, and lose faith in the chances of the startup to succeed. As leaders, you should never allow this to happen, at any cost.

So how can we ensure we foster *smarter* grit in our teams, to allow us to better survive the ups and downs of a startup lifecycle? An obvious first step is building a team with resilience. So ensure you're screening for that skill set in interviews (most interview questions should be open ended, including this). Then, practice what you preach. Identify important problems that need to be prioritized and solved. We can do this by applying the frameworks we have been discussing: critical thinking, statistical thinking, ensuring what you work on is tied to a well thought through mission and vision, considering level of effort, and understanding trade-offs and secondary and tertiary effects. For example, knowing that a problem does not align with your strategy and doesn't fundamentally help the current priorities, and seems to have a lot of unknowns and a high level of effort, seems to be a good candidate to bury in the backlog somewhere.

After identifying *true* priorities, attack them in organized and persistent ways, and don't give up after just one or two tries. Sometimes, you will have to pick the best of several bad solutions with some terrible trade-offs, but there is always a solution somewhere. Applying grit to the problem and going through several iterations may reveal a great solution that no one ever thought of, but you won't be able to arrive there without sticking with problems for longer.

Then, ensure you are delegating and mentoring others to stick with problems. Reward and celebrate those that solve big, tough problems for the organization. Set context: help people connect a great outcome to a tough problem being solved. Revenue trajectory could have changed, another channel may have been opened, customers raved and gave testimonials, or you may be attracting more investment interest. And as you see some consistency to decision making, good outcomes, and team persistence, just continue to add stability, positive reinforcement, and good processes, and grit will become ingrained in your company's DNA.

CHAPTER 9:
MAKING BIG BETS

T hinking about product vision with a long term view raises your chances of achieving something big. Those focused on short term views may win some battles and stay alive, but will ultimately be innovated away by future thinkers. A decade, in fact, is a good timeframe for thinking about product vision. What is the logical conclusion to what you're building? If you're one of your own users, 10 years from now, what's missing? What problems need to be solved? What did your competitors completely miss? Thinking about problems in a future state may help you see innovations that you couldn't see before.

And the reason why innovations are important, is that if all competitors just built the same thing, every solution becomes commoditized. The only differentiator will be price, and perhaps how good your sales and marketing teams are. But everyone will eventually realize there is no difference between your solution and everyone else's, and it will just become a race to the bottom for lowest price. Crowded markets with cloned solutions are not a fun place to be, so how can you stand out from the competitive herd?

The Moneymaker Effect

Against all odds, the accountant from Tennessee was one opponent away from winning the 2003 World Series of Poker. He had already outlasted 837 players, many of them professionals, and needed to beat just one more to become world champion, and turn an $86 entry fee into a $2.5 million dollar payout. He wore a beige baseball cap pulled tightly over his brow, and a pair of Oakley sunglasses that shielded his eyes from view. He had the same rigid facial expression on every hand, giving off the demeanor of a statue. However, it felt more like the accountant was holding his breath during hands rather than actually trying to intimidate his opponents, but he seemed to be holding his own against the top professionals in the game.

The final two players were surrounded by cameras and a crowd of family, friends, media, and random poker fans. The player on the other side of the table was Sammy Farha, a seasoned professional poker player known for his table talk and unsettling ability to read his opponents. He was also a guy that didn't seem to like folding hands very much, which made him incredibly difficult to bluff. Moneymaker held a small chip advantage over his opponent, 4.6 million chips to Sammy's 3.7 million.

The accountant had just raised 800,000 chips into Sammy on the turn with a flush draw and a straight draw, meaning he didn't have a "made" hand yet. The board was 9♠ 2♦ 6♠ 8♠, and Moneymaker had the K♠ 7♥, which meant he had to improve to win the hand. Sammy had the Q♠ 9♥, for a top pair (nines), which was a strong hand, and not one that many would fold here. Sammy calls the raise.

The river was the 3♥, making the final board 9♠ 2♦ 6♠ 8♠ 3♥, leaving Moneymaker with just King high. He had missed everything, and knew Sammy had the better hand. Most players in this situation, especially when you are the last two people left in the main event, might just give up here, and check. But Moneymaker instead ran a bluff that changed the poker world forever. He calmly looked at his chips, back up at his opponent, and quietly said, "I'm all in". This sent Sammy into the "tank", meaning he had to sit and think through what just happened before making a decision. If Sammy called and guessed correctly, he would be a huge favorite to win the tournament. If he guessed incorrectly, he would be out of the tournament in second place. "You must have missed your flush, huh?", Sammy said to the accountant, looking for a reaction. He was actually spot on. Moneymaker didn't flinch–it seemed like he had been holding his breath for over a minute. After a little more banter, Sammy did eventually fold, leading Moneymaker to let out a muted sigh of relief. After this big bet on this big hand, where Moneymaker risked it all on a bluff, he would go on to win the main event.

But why was this such an important event for poker? Back in 2003, poker was still not a mainstream sport. Throughout the 90's, the top prize in the WSOP main event was $1 million. In 2002 and 2003, first place had doubled to $2 million and $2.5 million respectively. Up to this point, pretty much every winner had been a professional or semi-professional poker player. Chris Moneymaker was the first pure amateur to claim the title, and he won his way in for only $86, when the tournament buy-in was $10,000. Moneymaker had shown the world that anyone could win. And this set off a poker boom. You can see the "Moneymaker effect" on the first place prizes after 2003:

1. 1998 - $1 million
2. 1999 - $1 million
3. 2000 - $1.5 million
4. 2001 - $1.5 million
5. 2002 - $2 million
6. 2003 - $2.5 million

7. 2004 - $5 million
8. 2005 - $7.5 million
9. 2006 - $12 million

Moneymaker had created an explosion of interest in poker, and his effect lasts even to today. Poker had a setback in 2006-2007 over the legality of online poker in the US, but since then, first place for the WSOP main event has hovered around $8 - $10 million for first place. And it all started with a big bet against a tough player that many others may not have been able to make. Your ability to make big bets can be the difference between mediocrity and being buried within the competitive herd, to achieving greatness and building something that might change the world.

The Importance Of Innovation

Most of the biggest returns on investment come from spotting an inefficiency in a market. Or in other words, seeing something that other people didn't see. To capitalize on these kinds of opportunities, it means you are taking a risk. If all the information were available, there is no inefficiency to uncover, and thus, no risk. But risk isn't so bad, as we learned in an earlier chapter about a framework for taking calculated risks, and deploying probabilistic thinking to make better predictions.

So where do you look for these inefficiencies?

Often, they are hidden in the blind spots of those with strongly held convictions and beliefs. When the masses see the world in a particular way, very few people have the ingenuity and foresight to see things differently. This is why those that can see the world in contrarian ways are often the same people that can come up with true innovations. Contrarians can be oddballs, and some of the things they say will not make any sense. But you cannot innovate unless you think differently, and this is what thinking differently looks like. And some of those ideas that are way out in outer space, can add the benefit of making you look at problems with different angles. From this vantage point though, perhaps a different solution can emerge, which would not have been possible unless you were looking at the world at very odd angles. To be a contrarian thinker that thinks so differently, you have to be prepared to have your ideas shot down. If people are laughing at your ideas, or trying to explain to you why they won't work, you're probably on the right track to building something innovative. Dream big, and ignore the professional critics.

Sometimes even very smart people will not see the vision of what you're trying to build, and this can be extremely demoralizing, especially when speaking with domain experts. But don't get discouraged. Most of the easy and non-controversial solutions are built already. And smart people can get ingrained in the status quo, just like everyone else. Sometimes, they can be *more* ingrained than everyone else. And in this environment, Incremental thinking abounds. When you challenge norms, you will sometimes run into those domain experts who just can't see the world a different way. To them, *things just work this way*.

But If you have an idea with a long term vision that seeks to solve problems for users in a new way, bet on that idea–and bet on yourself. You'll never know if you don't try. And if you can find those innovations hidden in dark shadows, ideas that make people laugh at you, you may have the beginnings of a moat that competitors will have a very difficult time trying to overcome. Riders taking cab rides with strangers in their own cars. Going on vacation and renting out someone's home for a weekend. Mailing DVDs. A smartphone with no buttons. All of these innovations were attacked with different versions of "this will never work", and "that idea is insane", but persistence and grit, and believing in your vision all left them winners in the end. And those domain experts can come work on your idea instead.

Seek to solve problems for your users in ways that no one else is solving it. This can be doing things much more efficiently than others, such as Zoom. This can be taking an entirely different approach, like the innovative companies we have been covering in this book. And when incumbents figure out what's going on, sometimes they will try to lobby the government to stop you, like what has happened to Uber and Tesla. This is a great sign that you are on to something big. But almost always, these incumbents will get left behind in the dust if they don't try to keep innovating themselves.

While you should be generally aware of what your competitors are doing, you should never really obsess over them. Obsessing over competitors will often cause you to follow their products, instead of coming up with novel ideas for your own. When you innovate, competitors chase *you*. And by the time they figure out how to build what you did, you will already be innovating on the next thing. Your competitors may also not realize how difficult it is to get your innovation right, if you built something that was truly a moat. This can put them years behind you in terms of market solutions. So lead with your own independent, contrarian thinking if you want to build great products. Chasing after competitors is a losing game.

Let's go back to our risk / reward matrix:

	High Risk	Low Risk
High reward	You need at least one of these a year to be innovative and win	Attacking these persistently will equate to long term success
Low reward	These don't make any sense	You have better things to do

While innovations tend to sprout from contrarian ideas, there is another common attribute to most innovations: they will be *high upside, high risk*. Without high upside, it wouldn't really be an innovation, or at least it would be a useless one. Without high risk, everyone would be doing it. This is because markets are generally efficient, so all the high reward / low risk activities will mostly have been done already. The outcome then, is that most high reward / low risk solutions become table stakes that you just need to build, because they have become a necessity. And if everyone is building all the necessities, you get crowded markets and commoditized software. Very sad.

So the high reward / high risk quadrant is where your innovations are hiding. Take those high risks when others are unwilling to, and you can monopolize all the upside. Build it in ways that are hard to replicate, and you will have a moat. Then you can have all the upside to yourself for a long time, or at least until the government calls you a monopoly. Some examples of companies that built moats are Google with search, and Apple with the iPhone. While some competitors were able to claw back some market share over time, these moats dominated their respective categories for quite some time.

Your product doesn't have to be all innovation. And if it is, that might not be necessarily a good thing. A product is a collection of features that cohesively delivers value to users. Some features have to do basic stuff simply, but the overall product should be differentiated in some way. So you don't need to reinvent the wheel on everything. Doing so may imply different workflows than what users are accustomed to. And if *everything* is different, you may run into adoption issues. People like familiarity, so they may not adopt something that is entirely different, or at least it might take a lot longer to achieve mass adoption (crossing that chasm). So balance "standard" workflows with innovative features, so users don't have too much mental overhead trying to learn new things. Sometimes, the innovation itself might be too much overhead for users. In these cases, presenting users a "compromised" version of your innovative product that balances familiarity with contrarian ideas will tend to be more successful. It is better that users adopt a compromised version, than to not adopt at all. And over time, you can, with plenty of educational resources and thought leadership, carry your users, and the entire market, over to the true innovation you had in mind.

Planning Your Big Bets

So how can we make room for those high upside big bets by safely introducing something high risk to the roadmap? And how can we foster a culture of people who seek to find high reward / high risk initiatives?

Hopefully with the framework we have been building, the methods to perform critical thinking and problem solving are better understood, such that we can be more confident in our analysis of what is truly high upside. With that framework, we can also be more confident in betting, and focusing on the long term vision and the execution of good processes and decisions, instead of losing ourselves in short term outcomes.

First let's look at team building. Definitely seek to hire some subset of people who aren't in your same industry. Generally, a team full of clones will just build echo chambers, and areas where there is constant mass consensus will be the last place you will find innovation. Echo chambers not only think alike, but can sometimes shout down people with different ideas. People who are not veterans at a specific industry will think differently, and try to apply ideas from a different set of perspectives and domain expertise. They may even take ignorant approaches to problems which may not produce great solutions, but may trigger some thought exploration around a new idea space that might lead to a home run innovation. A significant amount of successful companies ended up in a slightly different space than they started in. Sometimes this works, and sometimes this doesn't. But it almost always brings a different perspective. Just make sure you still understand who your users are and what problems they need solved, even if you want to take novel approaches to solve them.

Then, with the right team in place and the right mindset, we can start focusing on execution. Your product roadmap should have a few big bets a year. And just like balancing your actual product, ensure your roadmap is not *all* big bets, or you might have a different set of problems. You need to definitely balance your innovations with quick wins and low hanging fruit to ensure you are creating a usable product, as well as providing your team motivation and momentum as they deliver things into production with some frequency.

Good execution is highly dependent on good planning. You must find ways to balance the tidal wave of different priorities coming from different stakeholders, from users, product, engineering, sales, marketing, customer service, and others.

Your job is to be able to granularly score all requests so you can maintain a relative priority ranking, then organize everything in a structured roadmap, and set expectations on when things will be delivered. You will also have to provide a healthy amount of "no's" to ensure your team stays focused on working on the right things. But you're not here to win a popularity contest–you are here to win over your users and beat your competitors.

Let's take a sample set of projects we'd like to accomplish in a year, with some engineering estimates:

Project	Team	Estimate				
Small Project A	Pod 1					
Small Project B	Pod 1					
	Pod 2					
Small Project C	Pod 3					
	Pod 1					
Big Bet A	Pod 2					
	Pod 3					
Small Project D	Pod 4					
Small Project E	Pod 2					
	Pod 1					
Big Bet B	Pod 2					
	Pod 3					
	Pod 4					

You can see your big bets will eat a lot of time on your roadmap, and different engineering teams with different estimates will be dependent on each other. You also have a stack of small bets to accomplish (all of which should be relatively high reward). How do we execute all this while keeping thrash down across teams, and reduce context switching and complexity cost?

You should stack your projects so teams end

up near the finish line at roughly the same time. This saves QA cycles on end-to-end testing, and also prevents code from sitting there for too long on a "branch". Here is a method to stack your projects so timelines align. We assume we want to kick off the year with small quick wins to show some progress and build morale early.

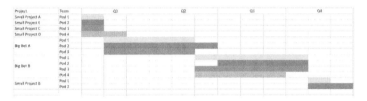

You can see how each pod can focus on one project at a time, which will reduce context switching and allow them to focus and finish more quickly. You can balance the end of a project (Big Bet A), to allow a smooth transition to the next project (Big Bet B) for individual pods, even if the timelines don't exactly end at the same time. You have also found some downtime for Pod 4 from March - May, which is a great opportunity to pay down some tech debt, work on another project, or share resources (if possible) to assist other pods. Similarly, Pod 4 and Pod 3 will have some additional bandwidth in Q4. This of course assumes that certain projects weren't time critical. But roadmaps can be easily balanced based on any number of factors.

It takes inventors and builders who can think outside the box to do impossible things. They are unafraid to challenge norms, and will often be irreverent and contrarian. Their ideas will be ridiculed, usually by people who are happy living in echo chambers. But the most important commonality for contrarian builders: their roadmaps will contain a few big bets a year.

So make room among the features that everyone is asking for, the bugs that need to be fixed, and the tech debt that needs to be paid down. Put a big bet that solves a problem for your users in a way that no one has ever thought of. Most importantly, surround yourself with creators who are optimistic and innovative. Be honest about your mission and your vision, and do your best to retain those who will commit to you. With a great team, you will motivate each other to reach heights you never could have imagined, and can celebrate together when those high risk / high reward projects come through with a big payoff.

CHAPTER 10:
TRUST THE
PROCESS

There is an interesting second order effect to the way professional sports teams run their drafts. Drafts allow teams to choose from a selection of non-league players, which are typically from colleges and semi-professional or international leagues. This is how teams build their rosters: they retain most of the players that are performing well for them, and then draft new, young players who will grow with the team. Finding a generational all-star with a draft pick can change the future of your organization. Lebron James, Michael Jordan, Kobe Bryant and examples of generational all-stars that delivered massive success to their teams upon entering the NBA.

Drafts work thusly: the teams that performed

worse during the season will get higher picks, which means they get to pick before other teams, and have a higher likelihood of selecting the best players. Those that can select in one of the top 3-5 picks in any draft can vastly improve their rosters in just a year or two. This causes all sorts of strategic gymnastics from the front offices of these teams that can frustrate observers, as the system can be gamed to try and acquire the top picks. But is it the system that holds the blame, or the owners who take advantage?

The Nba Lottery

As an example, the NBA uses a lottery to determine the top four picks in the draft. All the teams that did not make the playoffs are given lottery balls, with the most balls going equally to the three worst teams by record, second most balls going to the fourth worst team, third most balls going to the fifth worst team, and so on. So while you must still "win" the first pick in the draft, the worst teams will have the highest probability to do so. This is also a great example of the probabilistic thinking we discussed in earlier chapters: you are not guaranteeing a specific team gets a pick, or a specific card will be dealt next—rather, you are increasing or decreasing the probability that certain outcomes will happen. In this example, if I had to bet money on what is still an uncertain outcome–who will get the #1 pick in the draft–I would clearly bet on the team with the most lottery balls, and I would be happy with that bet, win or lose.

This lottery system is presumably designed to create *parity*, which means the best teams can't keep getting dramatically better by being able to draft the best players, while the worst teams should steadily improve because they *can* draft the best players. For example, the Cleveland Cavaliers were a bad team in the early 2000s, and landed the #1 pick in the 2003 draft, acquiring one of the best players to have played in the NBA: Lebron James. James dramatically turned Cleveland around to being a consistent playoff team within a few years, with very little support from other star players. Lebron went on to play for several more teams, and instantly added success wherever he went. He really is a once-in-a-lifetime talent.

But looking at how the draft is structured, you can see that this system introduces a perverse incentive: if you purposefully lose, you will increase your probability of getting a higher pick. If you are already in the bottom percentage of teams with no chance of making the playoffs, why not just lose on purpose so you can start rebuilding your team with the next generation of stars? And that was exactly the second order effect created by the draft process: teams began to "tank", or lose deliberately. In reality, this is not telling your players to throw the game, by missing shots on purpose or allowing the opposing team to score at will. But it does take some creative roster management and play calling to do correctly, while mostly staying within the spirit of competitive sport. And while this is not explicitly prohibited by the NBA, as it may be near impossible to enforce, it is very much frowned upon, because it's quite obvious when it is happening. The NBA is still a business trying to deliver a great product every night for their users: NBA fans.

While tanking can be perceived as an unsportsmanlike way of playing a professional sport, there is an important lesson to learn about *why* teams would choose to do this. They are taking a long term view for the strategy of their organization, and eschewing any short term successes. By focusing on a process of good decisions that are repeatable, and not focusing on just short term results, these teams would set up their organizations for potentially huge long term success, as they would be building a dynasty of young players, all hitting their primes at the same time. One team, and specifically one man, took this strategy to the extreme, leaving a trail of controversy in his wake.

Sam Hinkie And The 76Ers

Sam Hinkie was quite a student, graduating as valedictorian of his high school, and *summa cum laude* from the University of Oklahoma, before going on to earn an MBA from Stanford[25]. During his time at Stanford, he was also advising NFL teams on draft strategies and statistical analysis, and working part-time for the NBA Houston Rockets, who have also been a heavily analytical organization under the watch of GM Daryl Morey. After graduating from Stanford, he joined the Rockets full time, getting promoted to VP in just two years, and EVP three years after that. Hinkie heavily promoted the use of analytics in basketball operations and strategy, and played a big role in acquiring key players for the team.

Hinkie joined the Philadelphia 76ers as general manager and president of basketball operations in 2013. On his first draft day, they traded away the 76ers' only all-star, Jrue Holiday, for another player (Nerlens Noel) and a top five draft pick in the 2014 draft. Over the following year, Hinkie continued to trade away all the 76ers veteran players for more draft picks, leaving a skeleton of a team, strapped for talent. The team finished with 19 wins and 63 losses, at one point in the season losing a record 26 games in a row.[26]

Surprisingly, the fanbase and the players themselves seemed to take the losing extremely well. The infamous phrase *"trust the process"* emerged, representing the long term process set in motion by Hinkie, even with optically terrible short term outcomes, that would seemingly lead to a big future pay-off. "Trust the process" became the rallying cry across the city and fans, spreading like wildfire across social media and the news nationwide, and making it on to t-shirts and other merchandise. All the while, Hinkie used his trades and accumulated draft picks adeptly, acquiring future stars at a rapid pace, including one of the key current centerpieces for the team, Joel Embiid. But the 76ers organization, apparently not on the same page about what they signed up for, and the NBA and other team owners, did not seem to trust the process, and they allegedly forced Hinkie out of his job after three losing seasons in which the team had just 47 wins to 195 losses.

The 76ers landed the #1 pick after Sam Hinkie's departure, drafting future all-star Ben Simmons, and found themselves back in the playoffs in 2017, and look to be a force in the league for many years to come. These successes completely validate Hinkie's process, while the current regime can reap the benefits of his work. But the city has not forgotten who was the mastermind and orchestrator, as "Trust the process" still lives on, as well as other sayings like "He died for our sins", made famous by Embiid on social media.

Credit: Twitter

Credit: Instagram

Hinkie penned a 13 page resignation letter on his departure that quoted various innovators and out-of-the-box thinkers, from Warren Buffet, Bill Belichick, Elon Musk, and Bill James. Hinkie's resignation letter also included this memorable quote:

> *We often chose not to defend ourselves against much of the criticism, largely in an effort to stay true to the ideal of having the longest view in the room."[27]*

Taking a long term view has been a common theme throughout this book. And we have seen how having an obsessive view of the long term, while not stressing short term results, will lead to big payoffs if done correctly. So it's fitting we conclude with a look at the long term view.

A Long Term View

One of the great things about poker is that on any given day, anyone can win. Even a complete beginner can get a run of good cards and crush a bunch of seasoned pros on a Friday night at the card room. But the pros, who practice all the habits and frameworks we have discussed in this book, will eventually win in the long run. And it's because they make good repeatable decisions that lead to good outcomes in the long term, without stressing over any bad outcomes in the short term. And some of the most elite pros are massive money earners, which has been their reward for always taking a long term view.

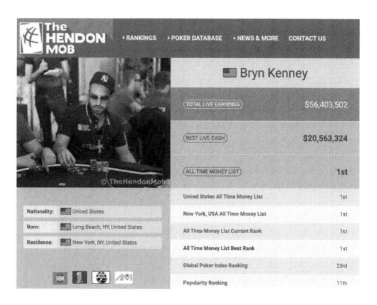

Bryn Kenney as of this writing is the winningest tournament poker player in the world in terms of money won, at $56 million. He had the single largest money win in a single tournament, for $20.5 million in the Triton Million event in London in August of 2019. These incredible stats might look like Bryn was some overnight success. But let's take a closer look at Bryn's numbers.

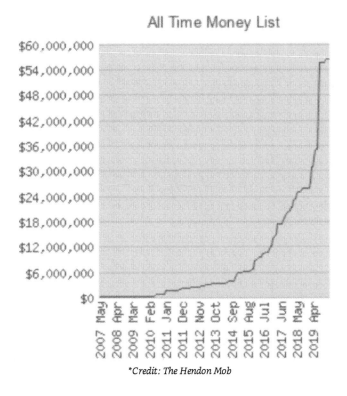

All Time Money List

You can see that Bryn had been grinding away

at poker tournaments since 2007. And his curve is quite the hockey stick starting around 2016, which was nine years after his first results. You can see how Bryn, like most of the best players and startups, are not overnight successes. It took Bryn over ten years to hit the number one spot in tournament earnings worldwide, just like Rovio was a "ten year overnight success" with their hit, Angry Birds.

But Bryn's graph also tells you a lot about how the best players in the world behave, and there are important takeaways for entrepreneurs. For a while, Bryn seemed to be figuring things out, learning as much as he could, and perfecting his craft. Bryn in particular has a unique and very aggressive style of play, which seems like something he honed carefully over the years. But as Bryn started to see better and better results, he started to play higher and higher stakes. Higher stakes means bigger prize pools, but also means much tougher players, as well as much higher risk of ruin, as you are playing for big buy-ins that can threaten your bankroll, even if you have plenty of investors willing to stake you. But Bryn was confident he had been making the right decisions, deploying a tricky and aggressive style of play that would lead to good outcomes. And as he saw success follow him year after year, he started to move higher and higher, until he eventually reached the literal top of the food chain. Bryn is clearly talented, but he also appears to be an extremely hard worker who exhibited years of persistence and grit. Follow the best startups around, filled with talented people up and down the roster, and you will notice they *all* have a strong culture of persistence and grit.

This is the mindset that entrepreneurs should take with them. Your first years as a startup are about learning and hypothesis testing, deeply understanding users and building things that delight them, and continuing to iterate based on their feedback and behaviors, as well as keeping an eye on some big bets that can allow you to innovate over your competitors. But really, it takes a while before you can truly hit product / market fit and feel confident enough to really scale. Like Bryn and Rovio, years of persistence and grit will lead to an eventual inflection point that will allow you to hit explosive growth. But you have to be patient to get there, and keep making good decisions along the way to keep you in the game.

It all starts with an aspirational mission, that is your company's North Star. This is followed by your strategy and vision for the product and company, which always ties back to the mission. From here is where you set your roadmap for the year and clearly define what your goals are, which ties back to your strategy. Then, in achieving the goals on your roadmap at a micro level, you continuously execute your strategy at the macro level, and each year keep getting closer to your mission.

*Most people overestimate what they can do in
one year and underestimate what they can do
in ten years.*

- Bill Gates

Having this big picture context, and thinking about your progress and goals with mission
and strategy in mind will build a culture of long
term thinking. And when the entire organization is bought in, then all your decisions across
the team will have a healthy focus on the long
view of where you're headed. Taking a long term
view really ties together all the concepts we have
covered in this book. Having an organization that
intensely focuses on the long term promotes:

1. Resilience against short term bad outcomes
2. Persistence in focusing on good processes
3. Future proofing your product and organization
4. Decisions made with big picture context
5. A mindset of trade-offs that considers
future impacts and opportunity costs
6. Forward looking attitudes even when in
the troughs of despair

We can put some examples to that list for

context. Imagine an organization that has a culture of thinking long term. This team would look cohesive–everyone aligned on mission and strategy. While they may complain they hear the same things over and over again in all-hands meetings, everyone also clearly knows what the strategy is. Their decisions seem more robust, in that when you test decisions secondary and tertiary outcomes (ie: what happens when x happens?), those outcomes seem to be accommodated for, and decisions seem to be future-proof and thought through.

The team decides to push forward with building a widget that seems to solve things better than any other solution in the market. It's also extremely different and high risk, but also appears to be the logical conclusion to where solutions are headed over a five year timeline. The widget fails to get adoption for several months after launch. What would the reaction of this organization be?

It would *not* be immediately reaching the conclusion that the widget was a bad decision. It would most certainly start with a long line of questioning, and not conclusions. And the questions would be less about the outcome, but about the decision, and also the execution of the go to market. An organization can default to this structure of analysis *only* because they exhibited all the traits of good decision making earlier. If an organization is not following a good framework, they will often be lost in the bad decision / bad

outcome quadrant, and unable to efficiently analyze what happened and move forward. This latter type of organization would be perfectly valid
questioning just the outcome, simply because the
decision was probably bad in the first place, so
nothing to analyze there.

The organization would realize the bet was
correct, so what went wrong? Was there not
enough familiarity and basic stuff? Was there not
enough knowledge leadership in the go-to-market? Should we have spent even more time with
our users? But we haven't budged from the vision,
at least not yet. These questions are all designed
to enhance the forward looking options: how do
we double down to make this work?

You can also see how solutions have big picture context: we didn't budge from the vision of
the widget, or the mission it seeks to achieve, so
all the tactics to drive adoption are *still* our steps
to achieve that long term strategy: to dominate
the market with a solution that wouldn't have ex-
isted for another five years. We are bringing the future to our users now.

Trade-offs will be making the product more
familiar, which goes counter to the vision, but is
a good trade-off to drive adoption, which may, in
a roundabout way, get us to our vision faster. And
if we hit more troughs, we'll be largely immune as
we're still laser focused on the long view. The long
view really does tie everything together, and you
can see how organized and efficient this team is, vs

a team that is full of reactive, short term thinkers.

We will leave off with some anecdotes from one of our generation's best long term thinkers, Jeff Bezos. This was in his shareholder letter from *1997*, when Amazon had 256 employees and ended the previous year with $15.75 million in revenue.[28]

> *We believe that a fundamental measure of our success will be the shareholder value we create over the long-term... Because of our emphasis on the long-term, we may make decisions and weigh tradeoffs differently than some companies... We will continue to make investment decisions in light of long-term market leadership considerations rather than short-term profitability considerations or short-term Wall Street reactions.[29]*

Fast forward to today, and Amazon earned $280 *billion* in 2019. Shareholders who stuck with Amazon through all the years of razor thin margins with the long term goal of achieving massive market share, have surely been rewarded handsomely for their trust. They all "trusted the process" of Bezos, just like the 76ers fans trusted the process of Hinkie.

Lastly, Bezos really does want to go "all-in" on the concept of long term thinking. He is of this writing in the process of building a 10,000 year clock in the mountains in Texas, which will... run for 10,000 years. Says Bezos:

Over the lifetime of this clock, the United States won't exist, whole civilizations will rise and fall. New systems of government will be invented. You can't imagine the world — no one can — that we're trying to get this clock to pass through.[30]

While this is certainly an eccentric thing to do, it underscores the importance of long term thinking when running startups as well as big businesses, and playing poker as a vocation. If we can train ourselves and those around us to take long term views on work and life, we will see benefits from the way we think, the way we do, the way we interact with each other, as well as collectively contributing to moving society forward into the future. But probably, we might need a little luck to get there.

♠ ♠ ♠

[1] MIT Blackjack Team (Wikipedia): https://en.wikipedia.org/wiki/MIT_Blackjack_Team

[2] Odds of 51 Random Events Happening to You (The Stacker): https://thestacker.com/stories/2343/what-are-chances#1

[3] Blockbuster LLC (Wikipedia): https://en.wikipedia.org/wiki/Blockbuster_LLC

[4] From HBR - How I Did It: Blockbuster's Former CEO on Sparring with an

DEREK KWAN

Activist Shareholder

[5] Netflix co-founder: 'Blockbuster laughed at us...' (The Guardian): https://www.theguardian.com/media/2019/sep/14/netflix-marc-randolph-founder-blockbuster

[6] The Making of Airbnb (Boston Hospitality Review): https://www.bu.edu/bhr/2016/01/08/the-making-of-airbnb/

[7] Taxi Medallion (Wikipedia): https://en.wikipedia.org/wiki/Taxi_medallion

[8] Uber, Lyft, and the hard economics of taxi cab medallions (The Washington Post): https://www.washingtonpost.com/business/economy/uber-lyft-and-the-hard-economics-of-taxi-cab-medallions/2019/05/24/cf1b56f4-7cda-11e9-a5b3-34f3edf1351e_story.html

[9] Uber (Wikipedia): https://en.wikipedia.org/wiki/Uber

[10] Micromultinationals Will Run the World (Foreign Policy): https://foreignpolicy.com/2011/08/15/micromultinationals-will-run-the-world/

[11] Behind the 2018 U.S. Midterm Election Turnout (Census Bureau): https://www.census.gov/library/stories/2019/04/behind-2018-united-states-midterm-election-turnout.html#:~:text=

[12] Ken Norton's online essay "How to Hire a Product Manager" will teach you just about everything you need to know about product managers.

[13] https://www.sec.gov/reportspubs/investor-publications/investorpubs-begfinstmtguidehtm.html

[14] How Google Wins Over Users By Giving Them Less (Fast Company): https://www.fastcompany.com/1672594/how-google-wins-over-users-by-giving-them-less

[15] Yahoo Memo: The 'Peanut Butter Manifesto' (The Wall Street Journal): https://www.wsj.com/articles/SB116379821933826657

[16] Worldwide desktop market share of leading search engines from January 2010 to October 2019 (Statista): https://www.statista.com/statistics/216573/worldwide-market-share-of-search-engines/

[17] Zoom CEO's Promise to His Wife Helped Inspire a $1B Company (Forbes): https://www.forbes.com/sites/peterhigh/2017/03/06/zoom-ceos-promise-to-his-wife-helped-inspire-a-1-billion-valued-company/#55c24f8e48a7

[18] Zoom Zoom Zoom! (Forbes): https://www.forbes.com/sites/alexkonrad/2019/04/19/zoom-zoom-zoom-the-exclusive-inside-story-of-the-new-billionaire-behind-techs-hottest-ipo/#60d0b9084af1

[19] The Dunning-Kruger Effect (Wikipedia): https://en.wikipedia.org/wiki/Dunning%E2%80%93Kruger_effect

[20] Angry Birds (Wikipedia): https://en.wikipedia.org/wiki/Angry_Birds

[21] In depth: How Rovio made Angry Birds a winner (Wired UK): https://www.wired.co.uk/article/how-rovio-made-angry-birds-a-winner

[22] The Inside Story Behind the Unlikely Rise of Airbnb (Wharton): https://knowledge.wharton.upenn.edu/article/the-inside-story-behind-the-unlikely-rise-of-airbnb/

[23] Airbnb's Surprising Path to Y Combinator (Wired): https://www.wired.com/2017/02/airbnbs-surprising-path-to-y-combinator/

[24] Greg Merson -- A Chip And A Chair Success Story (Card Player): https://www.cardplayer.com/poker-news/13735-greg-merson-a-chip-and-a-chair-success-story

[25] Sam Hinkie (Wikipedia): https://en.wikipedia.org/wiki/Sam_Hinkie

[26] Philadelphia 76ers (Wikipedia): https://en.wikipedia.org/wiki/Philadelphia_76ers

[27] Sam Hinkie Resignation Letter (ESPN): https://www.espn.com/pdf/2016/0406/nba_hinkie_redact.pdf

[28] A look back in IPO: Amazon's 1997 move (TechCrunch): https://techcrunch.com/2017/06/28/a-look-back-at-amazons-1997-ipo/

[29] Amazon 1997 shareholder letter (SEC): https://www.sec.gov/Archives/edgar/data/1018724/000119312513151836/d511111dex991.htm

[30] How to Make a Clock Run for 10,000 Years (Wired): https://www.wired.com/2011/06/10000-year-clock/

ABOUT THE AUTHOR

Derek Kwan

Bet, Build, Go is written by Derek Kwan, a startup executive and product manager who moonlights as a professional poker player. Derek has held product management positions at Yahoo! and AT&T Interactive, and is currently the Chief Operating Officer at Retention Science.

Printed in Great Britain
by Amazon

49686955R00109